Spiritual Classics
Series

Cover: River Windrush, Oxfordshire, England.
Photograph by Antony Edwards.

A Christian Woman's Secret

A Modern-Day Journey to God

Lilian Staveley

Edited by
Joseph A. Fitzgerald

Foreword by
Philip Zaleski

World Wisdom

A Christian Woman's Secret: A Modern-Day Journey to God
© 2009 World Wisdom, Inc.

Library of Congress Cataloging-in-Publication Data

Staveley, Lilian, ca. 1878-1928.
  A Christian woman's secret : a modern-day journey to God / Lilian Staveley ;
edited by Joseph A. Fitzgerald ; foreword by Phillip Zaleski.
     p. cm. -- (The spiritual classics series)
  "An edited compilation of Lilian's published books: The prodigal returns, The
romance of the soul, and The golden fountain"--Pref.
  Includes index.
  ISBN 978-1-933316-58-1 (pbk. : alk. paper) 1. Mysticism. 2. Staveley, Lilian, ca.
1878-1928. I. Fitzgerald, Joseph A., 1977- II. Title.
  BV5082.3.S72 2009
  283.092--dc22
  [B]
                                                              2008047764

Printed on acid-free paper in the United States of America.

For information address World Wisdom, Inc.
P.O. Box 2682, Bloomington, Indiana 47402-2682
www.worldwisdom.com

CONTENTS

Chapter 3. Contemplation, Union, and Trials

Chapter 4. The God-Force of Love

Chapter 5. The Romance of the Soul

Chapter 6. The Golden Fountain

FOREWORD

In *A Christian Woman's Secret*, the reader encounters a mystical confession both subtle and profound. Some passages bring to mind the fervor of Richard Rolle, others Jan van Ruusbroec's precision in delineating interior states, others the emphasis upon redemptive love of Julian of Norwich. All these writers date from the fourteenth century, and there is much in the book before us—its affective intensity, its devotion to the Trinity, even its preoccupation with the special spiritual life of women—that echoes the thought and culture of the late Middle Ages. But Lilian Staveley (c. 1878-1928) was a near-contemporary of ours, and in this lies the special value of her testament.

By all accounts, Staveley was a typical representative of the late Victorian and Edwardian British upper class. In his preface to this volume, Joseph A. Fitzgerald likens her to "a respectable lady shopping in London's Bond Street" for a "sensible pair of new shoes." She found those shoes, which we may take to symbolize a way of life shaped by boarding schools, fashionable balls, garden parties, Anglican services, and, finally, marriage to a Brigadier General in the British Army. But she also found something unexpected, a pair of ruby slippers that whisked her, via an intense longing first for beauty and then for God, far off the beaten path of ordinary lay Christian practice into a turbulent and ardent interior life. As a young woman she was briefly an atheist, but, she writes, "to a woman Atheism is intolerable pain: her very nature, loving, tender, sensitive, clinging, demands belief in God." She first tasted the divine through the raptures of landscape, spending hours gazing at clouds, trees, and flowing waters in England, South Africa, and Italy until she "assimilated and enjoyed inwardly the soaring essence of the beauty which I had previously drawn into my mind through my eyes." After a long course of suffering, during which she was prostrated by disease, struck by lightning, and wracked with fear as her husband went off to war, Jesus entered her life and changed it forever. Love of Christ supplanted love of nature. With this love came repentance and a long purgation, lightened by thanksgiving. Finally, through Christ, she came to the Father ("No one comes to the Father, but by me"—John 14:6). This culminating event, like the ecstasies of many visionaries, unfolded on a wild, deserted hillside.

The first manifestations were physical: "I was surrounded by . . . a great light or white cloud which hid all my surroundings from me, though I stood there with my eyes wide open." Blinded, Staveley felt tremendous energy suffuse her body. Then that barrier that each of us erects through sin to keep out God collapsed, and she cried out in joy, "so great was the force and the wonder and the delight and the might of it." Henceforth, until her death, she experienced the "*touch of God Himself upon the soul*" (author's italics).

Such are the lineaments of a beautiful and bright mystical life. The tale is compelling, and in the telling Staveley dispenses much good counsel, on the primacy of love, the indispensability of prayer, surrender of self-will, stages of metanoia, and the like. Her knowledge of the give and take between the inmost self and God is impressive. Here is a passage worthy of Pascal:

> The greater in prayer, the shorter in words, though the longer the saying of it, for each syllable will need to be held up upon the soul before God, slowly and, as it were, in a casket of fire, and with marvelous joy.

Alas, this high degree of lucidity sometimes eludes her grasp. Her intent can be obscured by purple prose, fashioned in exaltation, that paradoxically dulls her meaning. If Staveley had possessed a cooler, more analytic mind, she would have produced a classic. Instead, her writings have languished in obscurity for almost a century. She has had little or no impact upon the Christian mystical tradition or even upon its English-language branch. A few authors have recognized her depth; Evelyn Underhill, in *The Essentials of Mysticism and Other Essays* (1920), acclaims Staveley's testimony as the "purest form" of mystical love. But such tributes are rare. Thanks are due, therefore, to Joseph A. Fitzgerald for his judicious paring and rearrangement of Staveley's three books—*The Golden Fountain* (1919), *The Romance of the Soul* (1920), and *The Prodigal Returns* (1921)—into a coherent whole, bringing order and cadence to what are sometimes inchoate originals, and towards World Wisdom Books for bringing these rare texts back into print. Now Staveley's work can be read anew, as a worthy successor—aflame with beauty, framed in modern idiom but faithful to eternal truth—to the great mystical canon of the ages.

Philip Zaleski

PREFACE

Most of us, seeing a respectable lady shopping in London's Bond Street, searching, let us say, for a sensible pair of new shoes, are hardly likely to suspect that we are looking at a God-intoxicated mystic, comparable in her inner nature to a St. Francis of Assisi or a Sri Ramakrishna.[1] So it was with Lilian Staveley (c. 1878-1928). People familiar only with her rather conventional outer life little realized that she was one of the most remarkable mystics of recent times.

That the name Lilian Staveley is largely unknown[2] is no accident: the "white-heat" of her "spirit-living" was her secret treasure, the existence of which she divulged to none, not even to her beloved husband, Brigadier General John Staveley. Yet in three anonymously written books of a deeply personal nature, Lilian Staveley laid bare, for the benefit of fellow souls, the course of her own soul's journey toward God. It is the journey not of an unusual person "midway between men and angels"; rather it is the slow, up-and-down progress of a self-described "ordinary soul" possessing, however, extraordinary love for God and His creation.

In her autobiographical *The Prodigal Returns*, Lilian states that her upbringing was not typified by outward religious observance: "attendance at church upon Sunday—if it did not rain!—and occasionally the Communion." But her family's daily life was firmly based on Christian principles, and she possessed the simple—though somewhat fearful—faith of a child: God was a white-robed figure in the sky, who "took the trouble to make everything very beautiful . . . [and] could not bear sinful children."

---

[1] A bold analogy, though not unprecedented: in his book *Modern Mystics* (London: John Murray, 1935; reprinted New York: University Books, 1970), Sir Francis Younghusband explicitly compares Lilian Staveley with the likes of Ramakrishna and St. Thérèse of Lisieux. Younghusband also points out that the spiritual experiences Lilian Staveley describes bear "remarkable resemblances to the experiences of Hindu mystics."

[2] As mentioned above, Staveley's writings were known to Sir Francis Younghusband, a writer, diplomat, and Himalayan explorer. Her writings were also known to Evelyn Underhill, a respected authority on comparative mysticism, as well as to Frithjof Schuon, a preeminent writer in the Perennialist school of comparative religion.

Lilian's parents were people of leisure, learning, and culture who raised their children, Lilian and her two brothers, according to the same values. She experienced summers in Italy, tutors, governesses, boarding schools (Lilian spoke four languages fluently), and, when she came of age, a glittering world of balls, parties, and suitors. Of her first ball, Lilian tells us, "That night—and how often afterwards!—I knew the surging exultation, the intoxication of the joy of life. How often in social life, in brilliant scenes of light and laughter, music and love, I seemed to ride on the crest of a wave, in the marvelous glamour of youth!"

At the same time, despite the seeming paradox, she developed the ability to lose herself in contemplation of the beauties of nature. In solitude and silence, and with a view of the boundless sky, all thoughts and forms passed away, while through a process mysterious even to herself, she "inhaled the very essence of the Beautiful." It was a daydream in which, without fully realizing it at the time, she dreamt of God: "Half a lifetime was to go by before I realized to what this habit was leading me—that it was the first step towards the acquirement of that most exquisite of all blessings—the gift of the Contemplation of God."

But Lilian still had a long road to walk. Before she could find God, she first had to move farther away from Him. She became an atheist. An ardent, new-found belief in the truth and power of scientific "fact" replaced her belief in God Most High. It was a painful two year struggle for her to regain her lost faith, a struggle between her mind, which claimed that the God she had worshiped was a childish dream, and her heart, which nevertheless longed for His consoling presence. Faith finally prevailed over doubt when there arose within her heart a longing for her Lord so painfully real that the longing could not be denied. It happened to her while she was in Rome, in the presence of temples dedicated to the worship of an unseen God, and surrounded by the loveliness of nature. The beauty of worship, one could say, showed Lilian the way back to God.

Refinding faith was not Lilian's only struggle. She knew that many men, even otherwise great and holy men, have looked down on womankind, but, what was worse, she feared that in God's eyes also she was not of the "acceptable sex." This apparent disparagement she could not understand: "What profound injustice—to suffer so much and to receive no recognition whatever whilst men walked off with all the joys after leading very questionable lives!" For several years her shame at being a woman was such that, although she continued to believe in and pay homage to her Lord, she could do so only with a certain reverent sadness, and not with love.

The fullness of loving faith came to Lilian in time, as she realized that God, in His turn, does not differentiate in His love between man and woman. Despite the habitual arrogance of certain men, she came to understand that: "Clothed in the body of either man or woman, the soul is predominantly feminine—the Feminine Principle beloved of, and returning to, the Eternal Masculine of God." The spiritual journey of each soul to her Maker is a journey shared alike by man and by woman.

Lilian's writings unfold for her readers what to expect, step by step, along the soul's journey of love back to God. Her starting point is always her personal experience of that mystic journey. Outside of the Bible, she neither read nor relied on "religious" books.[3] She did not need to—with enraptured eyes she saw for herself the spiritual realities that the best books of wise and learned men describe.[4] That she never speaks second-hand may explain why Lilian's own writing is so often startlingly fresh and immediate in its quality of expression.

To whom does Lilian speak? To extraordinary monks and nuns who live apart from the world, or to ordinary men and women who live as a part of it? The answer must be that she speaks to both, but to the regular men and women of the world especially. With a natural sense of balance and harmony, Lilian teaches us how to combine an inner and hidden "blessed intercourse" with God, along with an outward life of everyday duties and intercourse with fellow-beings. To learn to live this "double life" took her time, but ultimately she discovered that love is one, and that sincere love of God must be combined with an equally earnest love for His human creation. For Lilian, such human tendernesses as charity and visitation of the sick are united in importance with heartfelt prayer and serene contemplation of the Lord.

[3] Lilian makes it clear that her understanding came neither from men nor from books; she tells us of two religious books that she did read, but these served only to confirm knowledge she had already possessed.

[4] Frithjof Schuon described Lilian Staveley as a "solitary," an individual gifted with a natural and, so to say, "spontaneous" understanding of the Divine who requires, therefore, no outside spiritual instruction.

The present volume is an edited compilation of Lilian's three published books: *The Prodigal Returns, The Romance of the Soul,* and *The Golden Fountain.*[5] The presentation is such that it can easily and profitably be read either cover-to-cover, or a passage here and a passage there, although the reader may wish to begin by reading the autobiographical passages contained in Chapters 1 and 2. Most of all, the reader is encouraged to remember that Lilian speaks directly from her heart and her wisdom is the wisdom of love. She is confiding in you her secret, the mystical love she carries within. Therefore listen to her with an open heart, as she whispers the sweet talk of love in your ear.

Joseph A. Fitzgerald
Editor

---

[5] Lilian's works are here presented in reverse order of their date of publication: *The Prodigal Returns* (London: John M. Watkins, 1921); *The Romance of the Soul* (London: John M. Watkins, 1920); and *The Golden Fountain or, the Soul's Love for God: Being Some Thoughts and Confessions of one of His Lovers* (London: John M. Watkins, 1919; reprinted by John M. Watkins, 1936, 1964, and by World Wisdom Books [Bloomington, IN], 1982). Editorial changes include the deletion of certain passages and the addition of new section breaks and headings.

CHAPTER 1

From Childhood to Visitation on the Hill*

Early Images

Sunshine and a garden path . . . flowers . . . the face and neck and bosom of the nurse upon whose heart I lay, and her voice telling me that she must leave me, that we must part, and immediately after anguish—blotting out the sunshine, the flowers, the face, the voice. This is my first recollection of Life—the pain of love. I was two years old.

Nothing more for two years—and then the picture of a pond and my baby brother floating on it, whilst with agonized hands I seized his small white coat and held him fast.

And then a meadow full of long, deep grass and summer flowers, and I—industriously picking buttercups into a tiny petticoat to take to cook, "to make the butter with," I said. And then a table spread for tea. Our nurses, my two brothers, and myself. Angry words and screaming baby voices, a knife thrown by my little brother. Rage and hate.

And then a wedding, and I a bridesmaid, aged five years—the church, the altar, and great awe, and afterwards a long white table, white flowers, and a white Bride. Grown men on either side of me—smilingly delightful, tempting me with sweets and cakes and wine, and a new strange interest rising in me like a little flood of exultation—the joy of the world, and the first faint breath of the mystery of sex.

Then came winters of travel. Sunshine and mimosa, olive trees against an azure sky. Climbing winding, stony paths between green terraces, tulips and anemones and vines; white sunny walls and lizards; green frogs and deep wells fringed around with maidenhair. Mountains and a sea of lapis blue, and early in the mornings from this lapis lake a great red sun would rise upon a sky of molten gold. In the rooms so

---

* Editor's Note: This and the following three chapters are taken from *The Prodigal Returns.*

1

near me were my darling brothers, from whom I often had to part. Beauty and Joy, and Love and Pain—these made up life.

Earnest Belief

I believed earnestly in God with the complete and peaceful faith of childhood. I thought of Him, and was afraid: but more afraid of a great Angel who stood with pen and book in hand and wrote down all my sins. This terrible Angel was a great reality to me. I prayed diligently for those I loved. Sometimes I forgot a name: then I would have to get out of bed and add it to my prayer. As I grew older, if the weather were cold I did not pray upon the floor but from my bed, because it was more comfortable. I was not always sure if this were quite right, but I could not concentrate my mind on God if my body was cold, because then I could not forget my body. I saw God very plainly when I shut my eyes! He was a White Figure in white robes on a white throne, amongst the clouds. He heard my prayers as easily as I saw His robes. He was by no means very far away, though sometimes He was further than at others. He took the trouble to make everything very beautiful: and He could not bear sinful children. The Angel with the Book read out to Him my faults in the evenings.

Of Parting and Dreaming

When I was twelve years old my grandmother died, and for three months I was in real grief. All day I mourned for her, and at night I looked out at the stars, and the terrible mystery of death and space and loneliness struck at my childish heart.

After thirteen I could no longer be taken abroad to hotels, for my parents considered that I received too much attention, too many presents, too many chocolates from men. I was educated by a governess, and was often very lonely. My brothers would come back from school; then I overflowed with happiness and sang all day long in my heart with joy. The last night of the holidays was a time of anguish. Upstairs the clothes were packed. Downstairs I helped them pack the "play-boxes," square deal boxes at sight of which tears sprang to my eyes and a dreadful pain gripped my heart. Oh, the pain of love at parting! there never was a pain so terrible as suffering love. The last meal: the last hour: the last look. There are natures which feel this anguish more than others. We are not all alike.

I had been passionately fond of dolls. Now I was too old for such companions, and when my brothers went away I was completely alone with my governess and my lessons. I fell into the habit of dreaming. In these dreams I evolved a companion who was at the same time myself—and yet not an ordinary little girl like myself, but a marvelous creature of unlimited possibilities and virtues. She even had wings and flew with such ease from the tops of the highest buildings, and floated so delightfully over my favorite fields and brooks that I found it hard to believe that I myself did not actually fly. What glorious things we did together, what courage we had, nothing daunted us! I cared very little to read books of adventure, for our own adventures were more wonderful than anything I ever read. Not only had I wings, but when I was my other self I was extremely good, and the Angel with the Book was then never able to make a single adverse record of me. And then how easy it was to be good: how delightful, no difficulties whatever! When, later on, I grew up and my parents allowed me to have as many friends as I wanted, and when I became exceedingly gay, I still retained the habit of this double existence; it remained with me even after my marriage and kept me out of mischief. If I found myself temporarily dull or in some place I did not care for, clothed in the body of my double, like the wind, I went where I listed. I would go to balls and parties, or with equal ease visit the mountains and watch the sunset or the incomparable beauties of dawn, making delicate excursions into the strange, the wonderful, and the sublime. I gathered crystal flowers in invisible worlds, and the scent of those flowers was Romance.

All this vivid imagination sometimes made my mind over-active: I could not sleep. "Count sheep jumping over a hurdle," I was advised. But it did not answer. I found the most effective way was to think seriously of my worst sins—my mind immediately slowed down, became a discreet blank—I slept! I grew tall and healthy. At sixteen I received my first offer of marriage and with it my first vision of the love and passion of men. I recoiled from it with great shyness and aversion. Yet I became deeply interested in men, and remained so for very many years. From that time on I never was without a lover till my marriage.

The Glamour of Youth
At seventeen my "lessons" came to an end. I had not learnt much, but I could speak four languages with great fluency. I learnt perhaps

more from listening to the conversation of my father and his friends. He had always been a man of leisure and was acquainted with many of the interesting and celebrated people of the day, both in England and on the Continent. I was devoted to him, and whenever he guided my character he did so with the greatest judgment. He taught me above all things the need of self-control, and never to make a remark of a fellow-creature unless I had something pleasant or kind to say. There was no subject upon which he was unread; and when my brothers, who were both exceedingly clever, returned from college and the University, wonderful and brilliant were the discussions that went on. Both my parents were of Huguenot descent, belonging to the old French noblesse. I think the Latin blood had sharpened their brains, and certainly gave an extra zest to life.

We spent the winter of the year in which I was seventeen in Italy, to which country a near relative was Ambassador, and there I went to my first ball. That night—and how often afterwards!—I knew the surging exultation, the intoxication of the joy of life. How often in social life, in brilliant scenes of light and laughter, music and love, I seemed to ride on the crest of a wave, in the marvelous glamour of youth!

Worship of the Beautiful
This love of the world and of social life was a very strong feeling for many years: at the same time and running, as it were, in double harness with it was a necessity for solitude. My mind imperatively demanded this, and indeed my heart too. It was during this year that I first commenced a new form of mental pleasure through looking at the beautiful in Nature. Not only solitude, but total silence was necessary for this pastime, and, if possible, beauty and a distant view: failing a view I could accomplish it by means of the beauties of the sky. This form of mental pleasure was the exact opposite of my previous dreamings, for all imagination absolutely ceased, all forms, all pictures, all activities disappeared—the very scene at which I looked had to vanish before I could know the pleasure of this occupation in which, in some mysterious manner, I inhaled the very essence of the Beautiful.

At first I was only able to remain in this condition for a few moments at a time, but that satisfied me—or, rather, did not satisfy me, for through it all ran a strange unaccountable anguish—a pain of longing—which, like a high, fine, tremulous nerve, ran through the joy. What induced me to pursue this habit, I never asked myself. That it was a form of the spirit's struggle towards the Eternal—of the soul's great quest of God—never occurred to me. I was worshipping the Beautiful without giving sufficient thought to Him from Whom all beauty proceeds. Half a lifetime was to go by before I realized to what this habit was leading me—that it was the first step towards the acquirement of that most exquisite of all blessings—the gift of the Contemplation of God. Ah, if anyone knows in his heart the call of the Beautiful, let him use it towards this glorious end! Love, and the Beautiful—these are the twin golden paths that lead us all to God.

A Fight for Faith
Certainly we were not a religious family. One attendance at church upon Sunday—if it did not rain!—and occasionally the Communion, this was the extent of any outward religious feeling. But my father's daily life and acts were full of Christianity. A man of a naturally somewhat violent temper, he had so brought himself under control that towards everyone, high and low, he had become all that was sweet and patient, sympathetic and gentle. About this time a devouring curiosity for knowledge commenced to possess me. What was the truth—what was the truth about every single thing I saw? Astronomy, Biology, Geology—in these things I discovered a new and marvelous interest: here at last I found my natural bent. History had small attraction for me: it spoke of the doings of people mostly vain or cruel, and untruthful. I wanted truth—irrefutable facts! No scientific work seemed too difficult for me; but I never, then or later, read anything upon the subject of religion, philosophy, or psychology. I had a healthy, wholesome young intelligence with a voracious appetite: it would carry me a long way, I thought. It did—it landed me in Atheism.

To a woman Atheism is intolerable pain: her very nature, loving, tender, sensitive, clinging, demands belief in God. The personal reason, the Personal God—these are essential to high virtue. Young as I was, I realized this. Outwardly I was frivolous; inwardly I was no butterfly, the deep things of my nature were by no means unknown to me. I not only became profoundly unrestful at heart but I was fearful for myself, and of where strong forces of which I felt the pull might lead me. I had great power over the emotions of men: moreover, interests and instincts within me corresponded to this dangerous capacity. I felt

5

that the world held many strange fires: some holy and beautiful; some far otherwise. Without God I knew myself incapable of overcoming the evil of the world, or even of my own petty nature and entanglements. I despaired, for I perceived that God does not reveal Himself because of an imperious demand of the human mind, and I had yet to learn that those mysteries which are under lock and key to the intelligence are open to the heart and soul. But indeed there was no God to reveal Himself. All was a fantastic make-believe! a pitiful childish invention and illusion! My intelligence said, "Resign yourself to what is, after all, the truth: console yourself with the world and material achievements." The heart said, "Resignation is impossible, for there is no consolation to the heart without God." I listened to my heart rather than my intelligence, and for two terrible years I fought for faith.

Towards the end of two years my struggles for faith commenced to find a reward. Little by little a faint hope crept into my mind—fragile, often imperceptible. That winter we again spent in Italy, in continuous gaiety amongst a brilliant cosmopolitan world of men and women who for the most part lived in palaces, surrounded with art and luxury. Here in Rome on every side was to be found the Cult of the Beautiful. Wonderful temples, gems of classical sculpture, masterpieces of color in oil and fresco—the genius and the aspirations of men rendered permanent for us by Art; but the Temples, those silent emblems of man's worship of an Unknown God, with their surroundings of lovely nature, affected me far the most deeply: indeed, I do not pretend that sculptures and pictures affected me at all. I was interested, I greatly admired—they were a part of education, but that was all. But in the vicinity of those Temples what strange echoes awoke in me, what mysterious sadness and longing, what a mystery of pain! Something within me sighed and moaned for God. If I could but find Him—if I could even truly Believe and be at peace! But already I had commenced to Believe.

Encounters with Holiness and Love
During the late winter we went to one of the great ceremonies at the Vatican: we had seats in the Sistine Chapel. It was an especial occasion, and the number of persons present was beyond all seating accommodation. To make way for someone of importance I was asked to give up my seat and go outside into the body of the great Cathedral; here I was hurriedly pushed into the second row of a huge concourse

of waiting and standing people. Already in the distance the Pope* was approaching. Lifted high in his chair on the shoulders of his bearers, he came slowly along in his white robes, his hand raised in a general blessing upon all this multitude. As he came nearer I saw the delicate ivory face—the great dark eyes shining with a fire I had never seen before. For the first time in my life I saw holiness. I was moved to the depths of my being. Something in my gaze arrested his attention; he had his chair stopped immediately above me, and, leaning over me, he blessed me individually—a very great concession during a large public ceremony. I ought to have gone down on my knees—but I had no knees! I no longer had a body! There was no longer anything anywhere in the world but Holiness—and my enraptured soul. Holiness, then, was far beyond the Beautiful. I had not known this till I saw it before me.

Life hurried me on: glowing hours and months succeeded each other. In the autumn I fell in love. I came to the consciousness of this, not gradually, but all in one instant. I had no chance of drawing back, for it was already fully completed before I realized it. I came to the realization of it through a dream (sleep-dreams were always exceedingly rare with me): on this occasion I dreamed a friend showed me the picture of a girl to whom she said this lover (he had been my lover for a year) was engaged. I awoke, sobbing with anguish. I could not disguise from myself the fact that I must be in love. When the time came to speak of it to my parents, my mother would not hear of the marriage—there was no money: I must make another choice. Two brilliant opportunities offered themselves—money—position; but I could not bring myself to think of either. Love was everything: a prolonged secret engagement followed. I went into Society just as before.

Mere Acceptance

The Faith that had been growing up in me was of a very different form from that which I had had before: wider, purer, infinitely more powerful, and, though I did not like to remember the pain of them, I felt that those struggling years of doubt and negation had been worthwhile—without those struggles I felt I never could have had so

* Editor's Note: Pope Leo XIII.

powerful a faith as I now had. God was at an indefinite and infinite distance, but His Existence was a thing of complete certainty for me.

Of the mode and means of Connection with Him I had no smallest knowledge or even conception. I addressed Him with words from the brain and the lips. An insuperable wall perpetually separated me from Him. Now my father became ill with heart trouble. Doctors, nurses, all the dreaded paraphernalia of sickness pervaded the house. During two terrible years he lingered on. Heart-broken at the sight of his sufferings, I hardly left his bedside. Finally death released him. But my health, which had always been good, was now completely broken down; I became a semi-invalid, always suffering, too delicate to marry.

Under pressure of this continued wretchedness I sank into a nerveless condition of mere dumb endurance—a passive acceptance of the miseries of life "as willed by God," I assured myself. I entered a stagnant state of *mere* resignation, whereas accompanying the resignation there should have been a forward-piercing endeavor to react out and attain a higher spiritual level through Jesus Christ: a persistent effort to light my lamp at the Spiritual Flame to which each must *bring his own lamp*, for it is not lit for him by the mere outward Ceremony of Baptism—that ceremony is but the Invitation to come to the Light. I had not obtained this light. I understood nothing; I was a spiritual savage. Vague, miserable thoughts, gloomy self-introspections, merely fatigue the vitality without assisting the soul. What is required is a persistent endeavor to establish an inwardly felt relationship first to the Man Jesus. His Personality, His Characteristics are to be drawn into the secret places of the heart by means of the natural sympathy which plays between two hearts that both know love and suffering, and hope and dejection. Sympathy established—love will soon follow. Later, an iron energy to overcome will be required. The supreme necessity of the soul before being filled with love is to maintain the will of the whole spiritual being in conformity with the Will of God. In the achievement of this she is under incessant assistance: in fact everything in the spiritual life is a gift—as in the physical: for who can produce his own sight or his own growth? In the physical these are automatic—in the spiritual they are accomplished only, as it were, "by request," and this request a deep all-pervading desire.

Married Life Begins

With recovered health, I married, and knew great happiness; but as a bride of four months I had to part from my husband, who went to the South African War.* Always, always this terrible pain of love that must part. Always it was love that seemed to me the most beautiful thing in life, and always it was love that hurt me most. He was away for fifteen months. I made no spiritual advance whatever. Mystified by so much pain, I now began to regard God if not as the actual Author of all pain, at any rate as the Permitter of all pain. More and more I fell back in alarm at the discovery of the depths of my own capacities for suffering. A tremendous fear of God now commenced to grow up in me, which so increased that after a few years I listened with astonishment when I heard people say they were afraid of *any* person, even a burglar! I could no longer understand feeling fear for anyone or anything save God. All my actions were now governed solely by this sense of weighty, immediate fear of Him. This continued for some ten years.

When my husband at last returned from the War we took up again our happy married life, and we lived together without a cross word, in a wonderful world of our own, as lovers do. It is remarkable that we were so happy, for we had no interests in common. My husband loved all sports and all games, whereas interest in those things was frankly incomprehensible to me. In the winter, when he was out in the hunting-field, I spent much time by myself; but I was never dull, for I could walk out amongst Nature and indulge in my pastime, if the weather were fine: and if not, I could observe and admire everything that grew and lived close at hand in the hedgerows and fields, and I would work for hours with my needle, for then I could think. A dreadful question now often presented itself to me: Had I really a soul at all, or was I merely a passing shadow, here momentarily for God's amusement? If I had an eternal soul, where did it live—in my head with my brain as a higher part of my mind?

---

* Editor's Note: The Anglo-Boer War of 1899-1902.

Existence of a Woman-Soul?
Men had souls, I was sure of that; and they asserted the possession of them very positively—but women? I understood Mohammed grudgingly granted them a half-soul, and that only conditionally. Scriptures spoke harshly of women; Paul was bitter against them; all the sins and troubles of the world were laid upon their delicate and beautiful shoulders. In Revelation I found no mention whatever of Woman in the life of the Resurrection. All this hurt me. What profound injustice—to suffer so much and to receive no recognition whatever whilst men walked off with all the joys after leading very questionable lives! Why continue to struggle to please God when His interest in me would so soon be over? I went through very real and great spiritual sufferings, and temptations to throw myself again solely into world-interests, to console myself with the here and now, for I had the means: it was all to my hand. I swayed to and fro: at one time I felt very hard towards God, terribly hurt by this love-betrayal. But when I looked at the beauties of Nature and the glories of that endless sky, ah, my heart melted with tenderness and admiration for the marvelous Maker of it all. Truly, He was worthy of any sacrifice upon my part. After all—for what wretched, ugly, and miserable men women frequently sacrificed themselves without getting any other reward for it than neglect and indifference. How much better to sacrifice oneself to the All-Perfect, All-Beautiful God! I finally resigned myself entirely and completely to this point of view, and, having done so, I thus addressed, in all reverence and earnestness, the Deity: "Almighty God, if it is Thy Will to blot out Woman from Paradise I most humbly assure Thee of this—Man will miss her sorely; and Thou Thyself, Almighty God, when Thou dost visit Paradise, wilt miss her also!"

After this I seldom said any private prayers, for I was not of the Acceptable Sex. But I paid a public respect to God in the church, where I worshipped Him with profound reverence and great sadness. But I thought of Him in my heart constantly, with all those tender, loving, longing thoughts which are the heart's bouquet held out to God. Happiness for me, then, must be found entirely in this world, and I found it in my love for my husband. Happiness was that which the whole world was looking for; but I could not fail to notice more and more the ridiculous picture presented by Society in its pretences of being the means of finding this happiness. None of its ardent devotees were "happy" people; they were excited, egotistical, intensely vain and selfish, often bitter and disappointed, filled with a demon of competition, jealous, and full of empty, insincere smiles. I perceived the chagrins from which they secretly suffered—the tears behind the laughter. I was not in the least deceived or impressed by any of them, but wondered how they managed to hang together and deceive each other.

More and more I looked for purely mental pleasures. Mind was everything. I now began to despise my body—I almost hated it as an incubus! Social successes or failures grew to be a matter of complete indifference to me, and social life resolved itself into being solely the means of bringing mind into contact with mind. The question of fashionable environment ceased to exist for me, but the question of how and where to meet with thinking minds was what concerned me: it was not an easy one to solve in the usual conditions of country life, with its sports and its human-animal interests. Finally, total mental solitude closed around me. In spite of my doubt as to the existence of a woman-soul, I still felt the same piercing desire and need for God—the acquisition of knowledge in no way lessened this pain. What, after all, is knowledge by itself? The light of the highest human intelligence seems hardly greater than the wan lamp of a diminutive glow-worm, surrounded by the vastness of the night. In sorrow, in trouble, in pain, could knowledge or the mind do so much more for me than the despised body? No, something more than the intelligence was needed to give life any sense of adequacy: even human love was insufficient. God Himself was needed, and the ever-recurring necessity would force itself upon me of the need for a personal direct connection with God.

I continued to find it utterly impossible to achieve this. Mere faith by no means fulfilled my requirements. God, then, remained inaccessible—the mind fell back from every attempt to reach Him. He was unknowable, yet not unthinkable—that is to say, He was not unthinkable as Being, but only in particularization and in realization. I could know Him to Be; but in that alone where was any consolation?—I found it totally inadequate. It was some form of personal Contact that was needed; but if my mind failed to reach this, with what else should I reach it? Ah, I was infinitely too small for this terrible mystery; but, small as I was, how I could suffer! Why this suffering? Why would He not show Himself? Harsh, rebellious, criticizing thoughts frequently invaded me: the whole scheme of Nature and of life at times appeared cruel, unreasonably so.

Bitterness and Disappointment

All the old ever-to-be-repeated cycle of bitter human thoughts had to be gone through again in my own individual atom. Here and there the bitterness might vary: as, for instance, the collapse and corruption of the body with its hideous finale never caused me distress. I had become too indifferent to the body; but I found that most persons clung to it with extraordinary tenacity, indeed appeared to regard it as their most valuable possession! What I did resent, and was deeply mystified by, was the capacity for suffering and pain which had no balance in any corresponding joy. It was idle to say that the joy of festivities, even of human love, equaled the anguish of grief over others, or the sufferings of physical ill-health. They did not counterbalance it; sorrow was more weighty than joy, and far more durable. Later I became convinced that there did exist a full equivalent of joy, as against pain, and that I merely had no knowledge of how to find it. Years succeeded each other in this way, bringing greater loosening of earth-ties, more abstraction, certainly no improvement of character.

My husband's duties as a soldier took us to many parts of the world. During a visit to Africa I was struck by lightning, and for ten days my sufferings were almost unendurable; every nerve seemed electrocuted. It was long before I quite recovered. Whilst this illness lasted, though it caused him no inconvenience and he led his life exactly as usual, I yet noticed a change in my husband's love. I was deeply pained, almost horrified, by this revelation of the natural imperfection of human love: profoundly saddened, I asked myself was it nothing but lust which had inspired and dictated all the poems of the world? I thought more and more of Jesus' love; I began to know that nothing less than His perfect love could satisfy me. In this illness I was tremendously alone.

My Jesus

I commenced to meditate upon the life and the character and the love of Jesus Christ. I was now about thirty-six. Gradually He became for me a secret Mind-Companion. I began to rely upon this companionship—though it appeared intensely one-sided, for at first it seemed always to be I who gave! Nevertheless I found a growing calm arising from this apparently so one-sided friendship. A subtle assistance and comfort came to me, it was impossible to say how, yet it came from this companionship as it came from nothing else.

That Jesus Christ was God I knew to be the faith of the Church, but that He actually was so I felt no conviction of whatever: indeed, it was incomprehensible to me. I thought of Him as a Perfect Man, with divine powers. He was my Jesus. I denied nothing, for I was far too small and ignorant to venture to do so: I kept a perfectly open mind and loved Him for Himself, as the Man Jesus. This went on for some years. In all my spiritual advancement I was incredibly slow! What had delayed me in progress was lack of using the right Procedure and the right Prayer. I sought for God with persistence and great longing; but I sought Him as the Father, and Godhead is inaccessible to the creature. On becoming truly desirous of finding God it is necessary that with great persistence we pray to the Father in the name of Jesus Christ that He will give us to Jesus Christ and fill the heart and mind with love for Christ. Only through Jesus Christ can we find the Godhead, and we cannot be satisfied with less than the Godhead. With the creature we cannot come into contact with the Godhead—but with the soul only. The soul is awakened, revived, re-glorified by Grace of Jesus Christ; and the Holy Spirit effects the repentance and conversion of the heart and mind, for without this conversion towards a spiritual life the soul remains in bondage to the unconverted creature.

Visitations and the Pain of Repentance
One day I returned from a walk, and hardly had I entered my room when I commenced thinking with great nearness and intimacy of Jesus; and suddenly, with the most intense vividness, He presented Himself before my consciousness so that I inwardly perceived Him, and at once I was overcome by a great agony of remorse for my unworthiness: it was as though my heart and mind broke in pieces and melted in the stress of this fearful pain, which continued—increased—became unendurable, and lasted altogether an hour. Too ignorant to know that this was the pain of Repentance, I did not understand what had happened to me; but now indeed at least I knew beyond a doubt that I had a soul! My wonderful Lord had come to pay me a visit, and I was not fit to receive Him—hence my agony. I would try with all my strength to improve myself for Him. I was at first at a standstill to know even where to commence in this improvement, for words

fail to describe what I now saw in myself! Up till now I had publicly confessed myself a sinner, and privately calmly thought of myself as a sinner, but without being disturbed by it or perceiving how I was one! I kept the commandments in the usual degree and way, and was conscientious in my dealings with others. Now all at once—by this Presentment of Himself before my soul—I suddenly, and with terrible clearness, saw the whole insufferable offensiveness of myself.

For some time, even for some weeks, I remained like a person half-stunned with astonishment. Then I determined to try to become less selfish, less irritable and impatient, to show far more consideration for everyone else, to be rigidly truthful: in fact, try to commence an alteration. And whatever my difficulties, I had always this immense incentive—to please my Jesus, tender and wonderful, my Perfect Friend.

Two years went by, and on Easter morning, at the close of the service as I knelt in prayer in the church, He suddenly presented Himself again before my soul, and again I saw myself, and again I went down and down into those terrible abysses of spiritual pain; and I suffered more than I suffered the first time: indeed, I have never had the courage to quite fully recall the depths of this anguish to mind. After this my soul knew Jesus as Christ the Son of God, and my heart and my mind accepted this without any further wonder or question, and entirely without knowing how this knowledge had been given, for it came as a gift.

A great repose now commenced to fill me, and the world and all its interests and ways seemed softly and gently blown out of my heart by the wings of a great new love, my love for the Risen Christ. Though outwardly my friends saw no change, yet inwardly I was secretly changing month by month. Even the great love I had for my husband began to fade: this caused me distress; I thought I was growing heartless, and yet it was rather that my heart had grown so large that no man could fill it! I felt within me an immense, incomprehensible capacity for love, and the whole world with all its contents seemed totally, even absolutely, inadequate to satisfy this great capacity. I suffered over it without understanding it.

A Gentle Song to God
I had a garden full of old-fashioned flowers, surrounded by high walls with thatch. As I grew in my heart more and more away from the

world, I worked more in the garden, and whilst I worked I thought mostly about God—God so far away and hidden, and yet so near my heart.

There were many different song-birds in the garden, and one robin. I loved the robin best of all. His song was not so beautiful as the blackbird's or so mellow as the thrush's; but they hid and ran away from me, whilst the robin sought me out and stayed with me and sang to me, all by myself, a little, tiny, gentle song of which I never grew tired. If I stayed quite still, he came so close he almost touched me; but if I moved towards him, he flew away in a great fright. It seemed to me I was like that robin, and I wanted to come close, close to the feet of God. But He would not let me find Him. He would not make me any sign. He would not let me feel I knew Him. Did He in His wisdom know that if He showed Himself too openly I should go mad with fear or joy? I could not tell. But every day as the robin sang to me in the garden I sang to God a little gentle song out of my heart—a song to the hidden God Who called me, and when I answered Him would not be found, and, still remaining hidden, called and called till I was dumb with the pain and wonder of this mystery.

A Pain-Song to God
Then suddenly came the Great War. My husband was amongst the first to have to go. All my love for him which I had thought to be fading now rose up again to its full strength: it was no mere weakly sentiment, but a powerful type of human love which had been able to carry me through fifteen years of married life without one hour of quarreling; its roots were deep into my heart and mind: the very strength and perfection of it but made of it a greater instrument for torture. Why should this most beautiful of all human emotions carry with it so heavy a penalty, for which no remedy appeared to exist? It had not then been made clear to me that all human loves must first be offered up and ascend into the love of God: then only are they freed from this Pain-Tax. God must first be All in All to us before we can enter amongst the number who are all in all to Him—constantly consoled by Him.

This condition of being all in all is demanded as a right by all men and women in mutual love, yet we deny this right to God: we are not even willing to attempt it! This failure to be willing is the grave error we make. Our attitude to God is not one of love, but of an expectancy of favors. An identical sacrifice is demanded of us in marriage—father, mother, brothers, sisters, friends: all these loves must become subservient to the new love, and with what willingness and smiles this sacrifice is usually made! Not so with our sacrifices to God—we make them with bitter tears, hard hearts, long faces. Is He never hurt by this perpetual grudgingness of love? But I had not yet learnt any of this, and I could not accept, I could not swallow this terrible cup. At least I was not so foolish as to attribute all this horror that was closing in upon the world to the direct Will of God: I could perceive that, on the contrary, it was the spirit of Anti-Christ, it was the will of Man with his greeds, his cruelty, his self-sufficient pride, together with a host of other evils, which had brought all this to pass. But could not—would not—God deliver the innocent; must all alike descend into pit? I tried to obtain relief by casting this burden on to Christ, and was not able to accomplish it. I tried to draw the succor of God down into my heart, I tried to throw myself out and up to Him—I could do neither: the vast barrier remained; Faith could not take me through it.

A horrible kind of second sight now possessed me, so that, although I never heard one word from my husband, I became aware of much that was happening to him—knew him pressed perpetually backwards, fighting for his life, knew him at times lying exhausted out in the open fields at night. At last I began to fear for my reason; I became afraid of the torture of the nights and sat up reading, forcing my mind to concentrate itself upon the book—the near-to-hand help of the book was more effective than the spiritual help in which something altogether vital was still missing. Relief only came when after a month a letter reached me from my husband, saying that the terrible retreat was over and he safe. Months and years dragged by. Sometimes the pain of it all was eased; sometimes it increased.

As grass mown down and withered in the fields gives out the pleasant scent of hay, so in her laceration and her anguish did the soul, I wondered, give off some Pain-Song pleasing to Almighty God. At first I recoiled with terror from this thought; finally love overcame the terror—I was willing to have it so, if it pleased Him. My soul reached down into great and fearful depths. I envied the soldiers dying upon the battlefields; life was become far more terrible to me than death. Looking back upon my struggles, I see with profound astonishment how unaware I was of my impudence to God in attributing to Him qualities of cruelty and callousness, such as are to be found only amongst the lowest men! Yet good was permitted to come out of this evil; for where I attributed to God a callousness and even an enjoyment of my sufferings, I learnt self-sacrifice, the effacement of all personal gain, total submission for love's sake to His Will, cruel though I imagined it to be. With what tears does the heart afterwards address itself in awed repentance to its Beloved and Gentle God!

God's Answer on the Hill
A painful illness came and lasted for months. Having no home, I was obliged to endure the misery of it as best I could among strangers. At this time I touched perhaps the very lowest depths. How often I longed that I might never wake in the morning! I loathed my life.

During this illness I came exceedingly near to Christ, so much so that I am not able to describe the vividness of it. What I learned out of this time of suffering I do not know—save complete submission. I became like wax—wax which was asked to take only one impression, and that pain. I was too dumb; I should have remembered those words, that "men ought not to faint, but to pray." Bewildered, and mystified by my own unhappiness and that of so many others all around me, I sank in my submission too much into a state of lethargic resignation, whereas an onward-driving resolution to win through, a powerful determination to seek and obtain the immediate protection and assistance of God, a standing before God, and a claiming of His help—these things are required of the soul: in fact that importunity is necessary of which Jesus spoke (Luke 11:7-9): "And I say unto you, Ask, and it shall be given to you; seek, and ye shall find; knock, and it shall be opened unto you." Such times of distress are storms, fearful battles of the soul in which she must not faint but rise up and walk towards God and clamor for help; and she will receive it. In His own good time He will give her all that she asks and more even than she dreamed of.

It was summer-time: a great battle was raging in France. A friend wrote me that my husband was up in the very foremost part of it. I heard no word from my husband; weeks passed, and still the same ominous silence. At last the day came when the shadow of these two fearful years rose up and overwhelmed me altogether. I went up on to the wild lonely hill where I so often walked, and there I contended with God for His help. For the first time in my life there was nothing between God and myself—this had *continually* happened with Jesus

Christ, but not with God the Father, Who remained totally inaccessible to me. Now, like a man standing in a very dark place and seeing nothing but knowing himself immediately near to another—so I knew myself in very great nearness to God. I had no need for eyes to see outwardly, because of the immense magnetism of this inward Awareness. At the moment my heart and mind ran like water before Him—praying Him, beseeching Him for His help; at another my soul stood straight up before Him, contending and claiming because she could bear no more: and it felt as though the Spirit of God stood over against my spirit, and my spirit wrestled with God's Spirit for more than an hour. But He gave me no answer, no sign, no help. He gave me nothing but that awful silence which seems to hang forever between God and Man. And I became exhausted, and turned away in despair from God, and from supplication, and from striving, and from contending, and, very quiet and profoundly sad, I stood looking out across the hills to the distant view—how gentle and lovely this peace of the evening sky, whilst on earth all the nations of the world were fighting together in blood and fury and pain!

I had stood there for perhaps ten minutes, mutely and sadly wondering at the meaning of it all, and was commencing to walk away when suddenly I was surrounded by a great whiteness which blotted out from me all my surroundings. It was like a great light or white cloud which hid all my surroundings from me, though I stood there with my eyes wide open: so that I said to myself, "It is an electric cloud," and it pricked me from my head down to my elbows, but no further. I felt no fear whatever, but a very great wonder, and stood there all quite simple and placid, feeling very quiet. Then there began to be poured into me an indescribably great vitality, so that I said to myself, "I am being filled with some marvelous Elixir." And it filled me from the feet up, gently and slowly, so that I could notice every advance of it. As it rose higher in me so I grew to feel freed: that is to say, I had within me the astounding sensation of having the capacity to pass where or how I would—which is to say I felt freed of the law of gravity. I was like a free spirit—I felt and knew myself this glorious freedom! I tasted for some moments a new form of living! Words are unable to convey the splendor of it, the boundless joy, the liberty, the glory of it. And the incomprehensible Power rose and rose in me until it reached the very crown of my head, and immediately it had quite filled me a marvelous thing happened—the Wall, the dreadful Barrier

18

between God and me, came down entirely, and immediately I loved Him. I was so filled with love that I had to cry aloud my love, so great was the force and the wonder and the delight and the might of it.

And now, slowly, the vivid whiteness melted away so that I saw everything around me once more just as before; but for a little while I continued to stand there very still and thoughtful, because I was filled with wonder and great peace. Then I turned to walk home, but I walked as a New Creature in a New World—my heart felt like the heart of an angel, glowing white-hot with the love for God, and all my sorrows fled away in a vast joy! This was His answer, this was His help. After years and years of wrestling and struggling, in one moment of time He had let me find Him, He had poured His Paradise into my soul! Never was such inconceivable joy—never was such gladness! My griefs and pains and woes were wiped away—totally effaced as though they had never existed!

Oh, the magnificence of such splendid joy! The whole of space could scarcely now be large enough to hold me! I needed all of it—I welcomed immensity as once I was oppressed by it. God and my Soul, and Love, and Space!

CHAPTER 2
A New Consciousness

A Walk in Eden

At last my little suffering life is sheltered in the known, the felt, protection of the Ineffable and Invisible Being. The Being Who, without revealing Himself to me by sight or sound, yet communicates Himself to me in some divine manner at once all-sufficing and inexpressible. I ask no questions: I am in no haste of anxious learning. My heart and my mind and my soul stand still and drink in the glory of this happiness. All day, often half the night, I worship Him. I love Him with this new love, so different from anything known before. The greatest earthly love, by comparison to it, has become feeble, impure, almost grotesque in its inefficiency—a tinsel counterfeit of this glistening mystery which must still be spoken of as love because I know no other name. I find it difficult, almost impossible, to speak to my fellow-creatures, because I have only two words, two thoughts in my entire being: my God, and my love for Him.

I wake with His name upon my lips, with His glory in my soul. In all this there is no virtue on my part; there is no effort; the capacity for this boundless devotion is a free gift. Coming immediately after my anguished prayer on the hill, it appears to me to have come solely on account of that one prayer—the previous prayers, struggles, endeavors of five-and-twenty years are entirely forgotten. I comprehend nothing of the mystery, neither as yet do I feel any desire to comprehend it; but in a world where only love, beauty, happiness, and repose exist, I walk and talk and live alone with God. Yet the war was continuing as usual, my husband was in the same danger, I became ill with influenza, my friends continued to die of wounds, my relations to be killed one by one; but in all this there was no pain: the sting, the anguish, had gone out of every single thing in life.

My consciousness feels to be composed of two extremes: I am a child of a few years of age, to whom sin, suffering, pain, evil, and temptation are not known, and yet, though knowing so little, I know the unutterably great—I know God. This cannot be expressed—merely, it can be said that two extremes have met.

This new consciousness, this new worship, this new love is for the Godhead. Christ is gone up into the Godhead, and I worship Him in, and as One with, the Godhead. For three months this continues uninterruptedly. Then Jesus Christ presents Himself to my consciousness. Jesus, Who led me to this happiness, now calls and calls to my soul. Immediately I commence to respond to Him. He is drawing me away; He is teaching me something—at first I do not know what, but soon I know that He is leading me out of this Eden, this paradise of my childhood: I know it, because I begin to feel pain again, and to recognize evil. O my Jesus, my Jesus, must I really follow Thee out of Paradise back into pain? Yes, in less than two weeks I am fully back in the world again—but not the same world, *because I know how to escape from it.* I can go in and out; the Door that I knocked at, and that all in one moment was opened to me, is *never closed.*

Living at White Heat

For three months I am walking further and further out of Eden and back into the horrors of the world—following Jesus. One night I compose myself as usual for sleep, but I do not sleep, neither can I say that I am quite awake. It is neither sleep, nor is my wakefulness the usual wakefulness. I do not dream, I cannot move. My consciousness is alight with a new fiery energy of life; it feels to extend to an infinite distance beyond my body, and yet remains connected with my body. I live in a manner totally new and totally incomprehensible, a life in which none of my senses are used and which is yet a thousand, and more than a thousand, times as vivid. It is living at white heat—without forms, without sound, without sight, without anything which I have ever been aware of in this world, and at a terrible speed. What is the meaning of all this? I do not know: my body is quite helpless and is distressed, but I am not afraid. God is teaching me something in His own way.

For six weeks every night I enter this condition, and the duration and power or intensity of it increase by degrees. It feels that my soul is projected or travels for incalculable distances beyond my body—(long afterwards I understand through experience that this is not the mode of it, but that the soul *remaining in the body* is by some de-insulation exposed to the knowledge of spirit-life as and when free of the flesh)—and I learn to comprehend and to know a new manner of living, as a swimmer learns a new mode of progression by means of his swimming, which is not his natural way. By the end of three weeks I can remain nightly for many hours in this condition, which is always accompanied by an intense and vivid consciousness of God.

As this consciousness of God becomes more and more vivid so my body suffers more and more. I am perfectly healthy, though I have hardly any sleep and very little, indeed almost no, food—the suffering is only at night with the breathing and the heart when in this strange condition. But I have no anxiety whatever; I am glad that He shall do as He pleases with me. Nothing but love can give us this supreme confidence. During the whole of these experiences I live in a state of very considerable abstraction. But this now suddenly increases, increases to such an extent that I hardly know whether to call it abstraction or the extremity of poverty. I now become divested of all interests outside and inside, divested of the greater part of my intelligence, divested of my will. I am of no value whatever, less than the dust on the road.

In this awful nothingness I am still I. My consciousness continues and is not confounded with or lost in any other consciousness, but is reduced to stark nakedness and worth nothing: and this worthless nothing is hung up and, as it were, suspended nowhere in particular as far from earth as from heaven, totally unknown and unwanted by both God and Man. I am naked patience—waiting. I have a few thoughts, but very few: I think one thought where in normal times I should think ten thousand. I feel and know that I am nothing, and I feel that this has been done to me; just as before, all that I had was also done to me and was a gift. One of my few thoughts is that I shall remain for the rest of my natural life in this pitiful state where, however, I shall hope to be preserved from further sinning simply because I have not a sufficiency of will, intelligence, or thought with which to sin! I have another thought, which is that as I no longer have any intelligence with which to deal with the ordinary difficulties of life, such as street life and traffic, I shall shortly be run over and killed; and so I put a card with my address on it into my little handbag, for the convenience of those who shall be obliged to deal with my body afterwards. I have just sufficient capacity left me to automatically, mechanically, go through with the necessities of life. I have not become idiotic. I live in a tremendous and profound solitude, such a solitude as would frighten many people greatly. But my beautiful pastime had accustomed me to solitude and also to something of this nothingness—a brief nothingness was a necessary part of the beautiful pastime: so I have no fears now of any kind; but I wonder. Perhaps I am just four things—wonder, patience, resignation, and nothing.

An Unseen Guide

Yet through this dreadful solitude penetrates the inspiration of some unseen guide. As regards this particular time I am convinced that this guide is an outside presence. I depend in all my goings and comings upon the guidance of this guide who proves incredibly accurate in every detail, in details of even the smallest necessities. If this guide is a part of myself, it is that of me with which I have not previously come in contact; and it is not the Reason, but far beyond the Reason, for it *divines*. It is then either a spiritual guide, companion, or guardian angel, or it is a power possessed by the soul herself—a foretasting cognizance, a mysterious intuition of which we as yet comprehend little or nothing, and which we have not yet learnt to command: it presents itself; it absents itself; but it condescends to every need; it is always helpful, always beneficent; it sees that which it sees before the event; it hears that which it hears before the words are spoken.

It guides by what would seem to be two very different modes: the greater things come by a mode altogether indescribable; but for the small things of every day I will take simple examples. I am abroad. Someone in the family at home is taken dangerously ill. I am urgently needed; but the trains are overcrowded, I am unable to get my seat transferred to an earlier date, I cannot let them know at home when I shall return: all is uncertain, all is chaos. I am painfully anxious, I am ashamed to say I am greatly worried: I turn as always to my Lord, asking Him to forgive these selfish fears and to help me. A little while later a scene presents itself to me—I see my own room, I hear the voice of a pageboy standing in the door and saying, "You are wanted on the telephone"; then I am at the telephone, and a voice is saying to me, "*Your train accommodation is transferred to Friday the 19th.*" That is all, because I am rung off. Five days pass. I am in my room, and the page is really standing at the door, and he says, "You are wanted on the telephone." I go to the telephone, and a voice says, "*Your train accommodation is transferred to Friday the 19th.*" That is all, because I am rung off.

Again, there is a young lay-reader, closely in contact with Christ; he has a wife and young child. The weather is bitterly cold. A picture suddenly comes before me of this family, and there is a voice saying,

"*He was gathering together the last little pieces of fuel when your present came.*" Immediately I understand that I am required to send coal to these people, and to do it at once without delay. The following day the wife comes with tears to thank me, and she tells me, "We were in despair; my husband's heart is so weak he cannot bear the cold, he becomes seriously ill. *He was gathering together the last little pieces of fuel when your present came.*"

Always in this mode of the guiding are the little picture and the exact words: all of it of the easiest to describe; but of the other and the greater guiding I do not know how to tell. It is sheer pure knowledge, received not in parts, pictures, or words, but as a whole and in a mode so exquisitely mysterious as to be at once too intricate for description, and yet simplicity itself!

So now, in the time of this strange abstraction and poverty, when the cinematograph of my mind is closed down, and with it the delicate mechanism which takes up, uses, and connects all that we take in by the senses, and which makes the world so real and so comprehensible, is become unhitched and disconnected, so that nothing in the world seems any longer real or possesses either value or meaning, and I stand before it all defenseless, seemingly unable to deal with it, utterly indifferent to it; then and now Reason may very well say to me, "You are in very great danger"; but I am not in any danger, because I am guided whenever necessary by some condescending sagacity far more sagacious than my poor Reason, infinitely more penetrative and effectual than any sense of eye or ear. I remain fully convinced that at this time, at any rate, it was an outside sagacity which guided me—truly a guardian angel. This period of intense abstraction, this strange valley of humiliation, poverty, solitude, seemed a necessary prelude to the great, the supreme, experience of my life. As I came slowly out of this poverty and solitude, the joyousness of my spiritual experience increased: the nights were no longer at all a time of sleep or repose, but of rapturous living.

Unbearable Rapture

The sixth week came, and I commenced to fear the nights and this tremendous living, because the happiness and the light and the poignancy and the rapture of it were becoming more than I could bear. I began to wonder secretly if God intended to draw my soul so near to Him that I should die of the splendor of this living. My raptures were not only caused by the sense of the immediate Presence of God—this is a distinctive rapture running through and above all raptures, but there are lesser ecstasies caused by the meeting of the soul with Thoughts or Ideas, with melodies which bear the soul in almost unendurable delight upon a thousand summits of perfection; and with an all-pervading rapturous Beauty in a great light. There is this peculiarity about the manner of these thoughts and melodies and beauties—they are not spoken, heard, or seen, but *lived.* I could not pass these things to my reason and translate the Ideas into words or the melodies into sounds, or the beauty into objects, for spirit-living is not translatable to earth-living, and I found in it no words, no sounds, no objects, and I comprehended and I lived with that in me which is above Reason and of which I had, previously to these experiences, had no cognizance.

There came a night when I passed beyond Ideas, beyond melody, beyond beauty, into vast lost spaces, depths of untellable bliss, into a Light. And the Light is an ecstasy of delight, and the Light is an ocean of bliss, and the Light is Life and Love, and the Light is the too deep contact with God, and the Light is unbearable Joy; and in unendurable bliss my soul beseeches God that He will cover her from this most terrible rapture, this felicity which exceeds all measure. And she is not covered from it. And she beseeches Him again; and she is not covered; and being in the last extremity from this most terrible joy, she beseeches Him again: and immediately is covered from it. My soul, my whole being, is terrified of God, and of joy. I dare not think of Him, I dare not pray; but, like some pitiful and wounded child, I creep to the feet of Jesus.

When on the following evening once more the day closes and I compose myself for the night, I wonder tremblingly to what He will again expose me; but for the first time in six weeks I fall into a natural sleep and know no more until the morning. Then I understand that the lesson is over. Mighty and Terrible God, it was enough!

In the light of these measureless joys what is any earthly joy? What are the joys of those vices for which men sell their souls, but soap-bubbles! The whole meaning of life, together with all the graduated and accepted values of it, becomes forever changed in the light of the knowledge of Celestial Happiness.

The World Becomes Paradise

Wonderful, beautiful weeks went by, filled with divine, indescribable peace. The Presence of God was with me day and night, and the world was not the world as I had once known it—a place where men and women fought and sinned and toiled and anguished and wondered horribly at the meaning of this mystery of pain and joy, of life and death. The world was become Paradise, and in my heart I cried to all my fellow-souls, "Why fret and toil, why sweat and anguish for the things of earth when our own God has in His hand such peace and bliss and happiness to give to Every man? O come and receive it, Every man his share."

And the glamour of life in Unity with God became past all comprehension and all words. Is life, then, a poem? is it a melody? I cannot say; but it is one long essence of delight—a harmony of flowing out and back again to God. O blessed life! O blessed Man! O blessed God!

One morning in my room I began thinking and reasoning about a wonderful change that I knew had crept all through me. If God should now come at any moment of the day or night and turn over every secret page of heart and mind, He would not find one thought or glimmer of any sort or kind of lust, whether of the eye, of the heart, of the mind, or of the body; and all in one moment I realized the miracle that Christ had worked in me, and the words came over my mind, "Though thy sins be as scarlet, they shall be white as snow." And I stood there, gazing before me, speechless, and the tears of a joy that was an agony of gratitude poured and poured down my face like a rain. I did not sob, I could not speak, and very quietly I took my heart and my mind and my soul and laid them forever at the feet of Christ.

Communion with God

One evening as I knelt to say my prayers, which were never long, because since the Visitation on the hill my natural habit—whether walking, sitting, working, traveling, or on my bed—had come to be a continual sending up from my heart and mind the tenderest and most adoring, the most worshipping and thanking little stream of thoughts to God (very much as a flower, if we could but see it, sends its scent to the sun).

And because this mode of prayer is so smooth and joyous, so easy, so unutterably sweet, in that during it the Presence of God laves us about as the sun laves the flower—so because of this it was only for short and set times that I worshipped Him as the creature in prayers upon its knees; but those few moments of prayer would always be intense, the heart and the mind with great power bent wholly and singly upon God. So now, this evening as I knelt and dwelt in great singleness on God, He drew me so powerfully, He encompassed me so with His glamour, that this singleness and concentration of thought continued much longer than usual on account of the greatness of the love that I felt for Him, and the concentration became an intensity of penetration because of this magnetism He turned on to me, and my mind became faint, and died, and I could no longer think of or on God, *for I was one with Him.* And I was still I; though I was become Ineffable Joy.

When it was over I rose from my knees, and I said to myself, for five wonderful moments I have been in contact with God in an unutterable bliss and repose: and He gave me the bliss tenderly and not as on that Night of Terror; but when I looked at my watch I saw that it had been for between two and three hours. Then I wondered that I was not stiff, that I was not cold, for the night was chilly and I had nothing about me but a little velvet dressing-wrapper; and my neck was not stiff, though my head had been thrown back, as is a necessity in Communion with God; and I thought to myself, it is as if my body also had shared in the blessing.

And this most blessed happening happened to me every day for a short while, usually only for a few moments. In this way God Himself caused and enabled me to contemplate and *know* Him; and I saw that it was in some ways at one with my beautiful pastime, but with this tremendous difference in it—that whereas my mind had formerly concentrated itself upon the Beautiful, and remaining Mind had soared away above all forms into its nebulous essence in a strange seductive anguish, it now was drawn and magnetized beyond the Beautiful directly to the Maker of it: and the soaring was like a death or swooning of the mind, and immediately I was living with that which is above the mind: in this living there was no note of pain, but a marvelous joy.

Slowly I learnt to differentiate degrees of Contemplation, but to my own finding there are two principal forms—Passive and Active (or High) Contemplation. In meditation is little or no activity, but a sweet quiet thinking and talking with Jesus Christ. In Passive Contemplation is the beginning of real activity; mind and soul without effort (though in a secret state of great love-activity) raise themselves, focusing themselves upon the all-unseen Godhead: now is no longer any possible picture in the mind, of anyone nor anything, not even of the gracious figure or of the ways of Christ: here, because of love, must begin the sheer straight drive of will and heart, mind and soul, to the Godhead, and here we may be said first to commence to breathe the air of heaven.

There is no prayer, no beseeching, and no asking—there are no words and no thoughts save those that intrude and flash unwanted over the mind, but a great undivided attention and waiting upon God: God near, yet never touching. This state is no ecstasy, but smooth, silent, high living in which we learn heavenly manners. This is Passive or Quiet Contemplation. High Contemplation ends in Contact with God, in ecstasy and rapture. In it the activity of the soul (though entirely without effort on her part) is immensely increased). It is not to be sought for, and we cannot reach it for ourselves; but it is to be enjoyed when God calls, when He assists the soul, when He energizes her. And then our cry is no more, Oh, that I had wings! but, Oh, that I might fold my wings and stay!

The Ecclesiastical Mind

Having come so far as this on the Soul's Great Adventure all alone as far as human guidance and companionship was concerned, and having for more than a year known the wonders of the joy of Union with God—which I did not know or understand to call Union, but called it to myself Finding God and coming into Contact with Him, because this is how it *feels*, and the unscholarly creature understands and knows it in that way—well, having come so far, I had a great longing to share this knowledge, this exquisite balm, with my fellows, and I desired immensely to speak about it, to know how they felt about it, if they had yet come to it, or how far on the way they were to it, because I was all filled with the beauty of it, as lovers are filled with the beauty of their love. But I was frightened to speak to them, something held me back: also they felt to me to be so exceedingly full of the merest trifles—clothes and tea parties and fashionable friends; and each time I tried to speak, in some mysterious way I found myself stopped.

So I thought that I would speak to a friend that I had in the Church. Several times I had heard him preach very beautiful sermons, and I felt

I very greatly needed the guidance of *someone who knew*. I knew that I was in the hands of the God Whom for so many years I had so passionately sought; but He was so immeasurably great, and I so pitifully small, and I needed a human being—someone to whom I might speak about God. Yet I said only a few words, of the joy of finding and loving God, and immediately my friend spoke very severely of persons who imagined they had found, and loved, God. God was not to be found by our puny, shifting, and uncertain love: He was to be found by duty, by obedience to Church rules, by pious attendance *At Church*. He explained to me various dogmas which helped me no more than the moaning of the wind; he explained the absolute necessity (for salvation) of certain beliefs and written sentences, and ceremonials in the Church. Love was not the way. Love was emotion, emotion was deceptive: the mind, and severe firm attention to the dictates of The Church was what was required; in fact, he unfolded before me the Ecclesiastical Mind.

I shrank back from it, dismayed, frightened. Were all the deep needs and requirements of the soul to be satisfied in the singing of hymns and Te Deum, in the close and reverent attention to the Ceremonies before the altar, and of the actions of Priests! No; a total change of *character* was needed, and Christ Himself was necessary for this change—Jesus Christ gliding into the heart and mind and soul, and *biding* there because of that heart's, that mind's, invitation to, and love for, Him. Secretly—in one's own chamber, every hour of the day, in the streets, in the fields—in this way it might be accomplished. With Christ biding in the heart all the Church service would *become* a thing of beauty as between the Soul and God; but without this Jesus Christ dwelling in the heart, the connection was not yet made between the Soul—the servant—and the Godhead.

Perhaps amongst Romans I should find the understanding that I looked for. I had a friend, a Dominican: I approached him, and I could see that for (as he thought) my own good he longed to convert me to the Roman Church: it did not seem that he wanted, or by any means knew how, to bring me into contact with God. "Does anyone," I asked him, "love God with all their heart, and mind, and soul, and strength?" "No," said he, "that is hardly possible—what is required is—"; and here he gave me once more the contents of the Ecclesiastical Mind: more authoritatively, more positively; but he spoke as I now commenced to realize all Churchmen would speak—that is to say, as persons having learnt by study, by careful rule and rote, by paper-knowledge, that which can only be learnt in the spirit direct from God. How immense is the difference to the Soul between this knowledge that comes of the spirit and the knowledge that comes of study—the knowledge which too easily becomes mechanical religion! I thought of the beautiful and gracious simplicity of the knowledge that Christ gives to the soul: I saw the nature of the sore disease that afflicts the soul of Christ's Church, I saw also a terrible pain for Christ in all this of which I had previously been unaware.

A Hermit and a Nun

I was thrown back and into myself by it all, and into a great loneliness as far as my fellow-beings were concerned. Yet I continued to need to share Christ with humanity, piercingly, pressingly. I would go to a library and find a book—but, on the other hand, I did not know the name of a single religious book or writer. So I wrote my need to a friend, and she sent me the life of one, Angela of Foligno.* This book was a great delight to me, because, though written in tiresome mediaeval language, it yet expressed and shared exactly what I also knew and loved, and folded in strange wrappings of the fashion of the thought of long ago lay the same exquisite jewel that I also knew—the pearl for which men gladly sell all that they have in order to keep it—the knowledge of the Secret of the Kingdom of Heaven, of the Union of the Soul with God. A few months went by, and I wrote asking for another book, and this time came Richard Rolle** to my acquaintance—a little dried-up hermit, a holy man too, though I noticed how very discourteous he was to women; severe, critical, and suspicious, merely because they were women. How often I noticed this peculiarity, both in the monks of today with their averted eyes, as if the shadow of a woman falling on them were pollution, and long ago, Paul, and Peter also, and Moses, and many others, showed surprising weakness of intolerance and harsh judgment against Woman! Where was Wisdom in all this? Surely it was Folly flaunting and laughing and dressing herself cunningly to deceive, for did none of

* Editor's Note: Angela of Foligno (c. 1248-1309).

** Editor's Note: Richard Rolle (c. 1290-1349).

these men, from Adam downwards—did they never come to know themselves well enough to see that their danger lay not in the Woman, but in their own *inclination to sin*!

But this Richard Rolle, this person so discourteous to some fellow-beings, could all the same be very tender and loving towards God: he, too, held in his heart the Pearl without Price. He, too, knew that marvelous incense of the heart to God—that song of the soul, and called it by the same name as I. Oh, how intimately I knew those two people of centuries ago, and how intimately they knew me! A strange trio we made—he, the little wizened English hermit; she, the Italian woman in her nun's habit; and I in my modern Bond Street clothes: outwardly we were indeed incongruous, we had no links, but inwardly we were bound together by bonds of the purest gold.

Of whether my friend sent me another book or not I cannot be sure; but my interest was becoming altogether removed from the past, because Christ was pressing me more and more to the present and the living.

To Live Tremendously

Countless ages ago—who can count them?—the soul, born in a palace, has deliberately willed and chosen to become the Wanderer, the Street Walker; therefore fold up self-pity and lay it aside, because it does not live in the same house with Truth.

What is it that often makes it so much harder for the soul to re-find God when she is enclosed in the male body? Perhaps the greater strength of the natural lusts of the male: perhaps the pride of "Being"—as lord of creation; or the pride of Intelligence which says, I rely easily upon myself, I need no religion of hymn tunes, I leave hymn tunes to women, for the ardor and capacity of my manhood rush to far different aims. But can any sane man think that the Essential Being who has created the universe, with all its infinite wonders, and this earth with its beauty and its wonderful flesh, and so much more that is not flesh but the still more wonderful spirit—can any sane man really think that this Essential Being is stuck fast at hymn tunes (which are Man's own invention!) and knows not how to satisfy the needs and longings of that which He has Himself created!

Ardent and greatly mistaken Sinner, know and remember that to Find God is to Live Tremendously. O beloved Man with thy strangely vain and small pursuits and pleasures—thy pipe, thy wine, thy women, thy "busy" city life, thine immense sagacity which once in twenty times outwits a fool or knave—thy vaunted living is a bubble in a hand-basin!

Find God and Live!

CHAPTER 3
Contemplation, Union, and Trials

Everyday Woes

It would seem that lazily, reposefully, comfortably, easily, we can make no entry into the kingdom of heaven, but must enter by contest, by great endeavor. The occasions of these contests will be according to the everyday circumstances of each individual; the stress or distress of everyday life; for this is Christ's Process—to take the everyday woes and happenings of life in the flesh and use them for spiritual ends. What does the Savior Himself tell us of the means of entry into the Kingdom? He uses two parables—that of the loaves of bread, and that of the Widow, and both speak of persistent importunity. If we would find God, we must besiege Him. Of entry to Christ's Process first it is necessary that we try in everything to please Him: subjecting our plans, desires, thoughts, intentions, to His secret approval, asking ourselves, Will this please Him best, or that? Then the soul commences to truly know, and to respond to, Christ.

But she is not satisfied: she requires more. Woes may assail the whole creature: Christ offers no alleviation. He leads her straight into the woes: will she follow, will she hold back? The point to remember here is this, that whether we follow Christ or no we shall have woes: if we forsake Him, we are not rid of woes; if we follow Him, we are not rid of woes—not yet, but later we become eased, and even rid, by means of Consolations, for God is able by His Consolations to entirely overbalance the woe and make it happy peace, though the cause of the woe remains. Remember this in the days of visitation, and follow Christ, no matter where He leads. Christ leads *through* the woe, because it is the shortest way. The unguided soul wanders *beside* the woe, hating and fearing it, unable to rid herself of it, gaining nothing by it, suffering in vain, and no Companion comes to ease the burden with His company. The progress of our spiritual advance would feel to be that because we become more and more aware of the failure of earthly consolations and amusements, and more and more aware of the suffering, the sin, and the evil that there is about us, so more and more our desires go out towards the good, and more and more we turn to Christ. Then Christ may deliberately make Himself non-sufficient for the soul, and if He so does, she must reach out after the Godhead; then by means of more woes the soul and the creature clamor more and more after the Godhead and will not be satisfied with less than the Godhead, and, continuing to clamor, are brought by Christ to the new birth, the Baptism of the Holy Ghost.

Immediately the soul and creature become rid of Woe; and, living a life altogether apart from the world, in a marvelous crystal joy they taste of the Godhead and of Eternal Pleasures. This for a short time only: we have entered the Kingdom, but are still the smallest of spiritual children: tenderly, wonderfully God cares for us, but we must grow, we must learn heavenly manners. So Jesus Christ calls us again, and where does He lead us? Straight back into the world, the daily life from which we thought we had escaped! Here truly is a Woe, a Woe worse than any Woe we ever had before. Now we enter the Course of spiritual temptations, woes, and endurances, and in the midst of the pots and pans of daily life Christ teaches us heavenly manners.

All Can Contemplate

Since Contemplation is so necessary for Union with God and for the soul's *enjoyment* of God—is it a capacity common to all persons? Yes, though, like all other capacities, in varying degrees; but few will give themselves up to the difficulties of developing the capacity; and it is easy to know why, for our "natural" state is that we work for that which brings the easiest, most immediate, and most substantially visible reward. Those who could most easily develop their powers of contemplation are those to whom Beauty speaks, or those who are delicately sensitive to some ideal, nameless, elusive, that draws and then retreats, but in retreating still draws. The poet, the artist, the dreamer *that harnesses his mind*—all can contemplate.

The Thinker, *thinking straight through*, the proficient business man with his powers of concentration, the first-rate organizer, the scientist, the inventor—all these men are contemplatives who do not drive to God, but to the world or to ambition. Taking God as their goal, they could ascend to great heights of happiness; though first they must give up ("sacrifice") all that is unsavory in thought and in living: yet such is the vast, the boundless Attraction of God that having once (if only for a few moments) retouched this lost Attraction of His, we afterwards are possessed with no other desire so powerful as the desire to retouch Him again, and "sacrifice" becomes no sacrifice. Truly, having once known God, we find life without Him to be meaningless and as unbeautiful as a broken stem without its flower: pitiful, naked, and helpless as the body of a butterfly without the wings.

A Mystery of Eternal Giving

What is it that instinctively we look for and desire? Happiness, and the Ever-new. In and out of every day persistently, desperately, endlessly we seek. And because we seek amongst the near-to-hand, the visible, the small, we seek in vain: we discover there is nothing in this world which can wholly and permanently satisfy either of these desires.

God Himself is Happiness. God Himself is the Ever-new. In Divine Love there is no monotony: the soul finds that each encounter with God is ever new, the Ever-new tremulous with the beauty of rapture: new and wonderful as the first dawn.

Not only is God a Mystery of Holiness of Truth, of Love and Beauty: He is also Generosity, a mystery of Eternal Giving, and His giving is and must forever be, the supreme necessity of the Universe: for without He gave how should we receive life, truth beauty, love, or Himself?

And it cannot be too deeply impressed upon the soul that would come to His Presence that because of His law of like to like she must conform to His law in order to come to His Presence. By thinking it over we shall see that it is more difficult for us to be perfect holiness, perfect truth, perfect love, perfect beauty, than it is for us to be perfectly generous; it is easier for us to give God all that we have, to empty heart, mind, and soul, and worldly goods at His feet, than it is to reach to any other perfection; for generosity appears to be more universal, more within our capacities, more "natural" to us than any other virtue—do we not see it continually used, exercised, spent, thrown away on the merest trifles?

Let us take, for instance, the tennis player: to win the game he must give every ounce of himself to it—mind, eye, heart, and body—sweating there in the glare of the sun to win the game. Would he give himself so, in order to find God, or to please God? Oh no! Yet in the hour of death and afterwards, will he be helped by this victory of flying balls? If by chance we could lift a corner of the veil, we might catch a glimpse of the face of Folly, mockingly, cunningly peering at us, as all too easily she persuades us to give of our royal coins of generosity to wantons, to phantom enterprises, to balls·filled with air, to dust and vanity.

Generosity is our easiest means of coming to God, because it is also the way of love: if the tennis player did not love the game, he would not give himself so to it. But we cry, "I have nothing whatever to give to God; it is to God I turn in order that He may give everything to me." Quite so: there is too much of that. We have obedience to give: obedience is a great gift to God, or, more truthfully speaking, in His magnanimity He accepts it as such; we have also love to give, and again we may cry, "But my love is puny, shifting; it is nothing at all, a mere trifle." That is true of "natural" love, of the love that we commence of our own human nature to love Him with; but it is not true of the love which we receive of the Holy Ghost when He baptizes us. When we offer this Peculiar Love, offer it as only it can be offered—for love's sake—immediately we are in the Presence of God, secretly, marvelously united to Him; we are in the Consolations of God, and we have no need to ask for anything whatever; indeed, we find ourselves unable to ask, because we are filled to the brim, overflowing, inexpressibly satisfied, utterly blessed.

And if at times in the stress of this giving, when He makes no response, we feel it is too much, we can give no more, we are too discouraged to continue, let us remember the strain and stress and endeavor that we and all our friends give to trifles, and quietly use our common sense to judge whether in the winning of a game of ball, or in the pleasing and finding of God, we shall be the more blessed. For God is to be found: He waits.

Come and Know for Yourself
What I know of the soul's actual Finding and Contact with God I keep very closely to myself. Here and there to a few, a very few souls, I may speak: to all others I am forbidden to speak. I am stopped; and I understand perfectly why this is: it is that I should do more harm than good. Anyone looking at me would say (and all the more so because I am dressed in the fashion of the day, and not in some peculiar way, or in a nun's habit, for such trifling things affect many minds), "That person is demented to think that she knows what it is to have Contact with God," and it would seem a scandal to them. But the explanation of the mystery is not so simple as this. I am not demented. I never was so sane, so capable in my life as now. I never was so perfectly poised

as now. But if you say to me, "Explain what it is that you know, in order that I too may know," then I can say to you nothing more than, "Come and know for yourself, for God awaits you."

To illustrate a mere fraction of the difficulty of passing such a knowledge from one self to another self, let us take such a case as that of a man born blind. He sits beneath a tree, on the grass. You put a blade of grass in his fingers, and also a leaf from the tree, and you say to him, "This is grass, and this is the leaf of the tree which shelters you, and both are green." "And what," he asks, "is green?" And to save your life you cannot make him know what it is; or make him know the tree, or know the grass, though he touches them both with his hands. How, then, shall God, Who can be neither seen, nor heard, nor touched, how shall He be made known from one to another? He must be experienced to be known. And if you should say to me, "What does it feel like to have found God?" then I should say, "It feels that the roof is lifted off the world, and wherever we may be or stand it is a straight line from us to God and nothing between, nothing between, day or night."

The Way Is Not Denying

To come to the contemplation of God it is not necessary to go through any lengthy toil, some process of throwing out this or that, painfully, slowly, denying the existence of everything in order to arrive at God. The way is not denying, but concentrating; and in the act of concentration, because of love, all other things whatsoever in creation fall away into nothing and are no more, because God in all His graciousness reveals Himself, and then He alone exists for the enraptured soul.

Spiritualism Not the Way

The soul that is seeking Union with God must not, upon any pretext whatever, engage itself in spiritualism. Spiritualism may have its great uses for the heart and mind which are without, or are struggling for, belief—the heart and mind of Thomas seeking to touch, to have a proof; but remember the words of the Savior to Thomas: "Blessed are they," He says, "who have not seen, and yet have believed." And we do not need to wait for death to receive this blessing, but we receive it here. The soul that would find God must go to Him by means of His Holy Spirit, and no other spirit but the Spirit of God can take us

39

to Him; and to try to hold communications with the spirits of men *is not the way.*

The soul that has come to Union with God is perfectly aware of the existence of spirits—is intensely aware—but refuses to pay any attention if she is wise. Some of these spirits are very subtle, very knowing; some are full of flattery, and very persistent; others present themselves as still in human form, and seek to terrify with their terrible faces, some diabolical, some appearing to be in a great agony and undergoing changes more astonishing and horrible than can be even imagined before experienced. Have nothing whatever to do with spirits. Do not resist them when they come, but drop them behind by fixing heart, mind, and soul on Christ. The Spirit of Christ easily overcomes every spirit, every evil, every fear, and in order to ourselves overcome all such things, we need to unite with the Spirit of Jesus Christ by concentrating upon Him with love, and ignoring obstructions.

Mode of Heavenly Living

After coming to full Union with God, the mind becomes permanently attached to Him, *and this without effort;* but in order that it shall be without effort, the will must be kept in a state of loving attention to Him, and this again can only be done without effort if the heart is so full of love that it desires nothing else than God; and this is dependent again upon the grace which the soul receives from Him because of her love and response—so now we see, living and working in our own being, the reason and meaning of His commandment to love Him with all the heart, mind, soul, and strength. It is doing this *after He has Himself given us the power to do it* which makes us able to live in the closest, most delicious and precious nearness to God during all our waking hours.

But it takes time, and it takes much pain to learn how to live this, as it were, double life—this inward life of companionship, of wonderful and blessed inward intercourse with God, and the outward intercourse of the senses with the world, our everyday duties, and our fellow-beings. In our early stages we have profound innumerable difficulties in understanding either our own capacities or God's wishes: we are terrified of losing Him, and yet are often bewildered, and pained also, by some of the higher degrees in which He communicates Himself. We do not understand how to leave God and return to earthly duties. Supposing that we are altogether wrapped up in the company of God, and some fellow-being suddenly recalls us to the world (the human voice can recall the soul as nothing else can), the pain is so great as to be nothing less than anguish; and if done often would seriously affect the health of the body. But in a few years we learn to accomplish it without any shock.

One pain, however, remains, and it grows. I find myself unable to carry on a conversation with anyone unless it is about God, or about some work which is for God and has to do with His pleasure (and this is rare, because people are so glued to worldly affairs), for more than an hour, and even less, without the most horrible, the most deathly, exhaustion, which is not only spiritual but bodily—the face and lips losing all color, the eyes their vitality: so dreadful is the distress of the whole being that one is obliged, upon any kind of pretext, to withdraw from all companions, and, if it is only for five minutes, be alone with God and, where no eye but His can see, unite completely with Him once more, and immediately the whole being becomes revivified. There is nothing else in life so wonderful, so rapturous as this swift reunion of the soul with God; if this measureless happiness could only be imagined by us before we experience it, how many of us would be spurred to greater efforts instead of falling back amongst the dust and cobwebs of Vanity!

The soul which knows how to make all necessary preparations to receive Him becomes a source of joy to God, for now He can give and give and no harm be done to that soul; but He does not acquaint the soul too suddenly with all the joy that she is to Him, because she would not (at least certainly my soul would not) be able to bear the knowledge of the privilege that she enjoys, without some danger to herself—and so, all unaware of the singularity of the privilege that she enjoys without any analysis of her happiness, she concerns herself with sweetly obeying Him, with singing to Him, and with giving Him all that she has all the day long, and so hovers before Him as delightful simplicity and love. This Union with God varies so much in degree that it makes an effect of endless variety. Yet it is all one same joy, it is the joy of angels reduced to such degree as makes it bearable to flesh: the soul knows that it is the joy of angels that she is receiving the first time that she has it given to her: immediately on receipt of this joy she comprehends the *mode* of heavenly living; she knows it is but the outer edge that she touches, but what means so much to her is that she has *recaptured the knowledge of this mode of living*: henceforth it is a question of progress, she bends all her attention to progress so that she may get nearer and nearer to God, so that she may do everything to please this suddenly refound, unspeakably beloved God. She desires to get nearer and nearer to God in spite of the pain that she often experiences.

Perhaps the first pains we experience are when we are in contemplation of God and are caught by God into High Contemplation. He will at times expose the soul to so much of the Divine Power that she cannot sever herself from the too great fullness of Union with God, though the body is crying to her to do it and the sufferings of the body are all felt by the soul, which is pulled two ways: all this is very painful and makes us almost in a fear of God again. Why should Perfect Love inflict this pain on us? It may be to remind us that He is not only Love, but Power, Might, Majesty, and Dominion also. Yet could this ever be forgotten? It seems incredible. But it does not do to trust to one's soul, or to count on what she will do or not do: we know that the soul has forgotten almost everything about God, so much so that we are now thankful to arrive even so far as being quite certain that He exists! What infinite kindness that He should consent and condescend to Himself be her Teacher!

Marriage-Union and God-Union

When the soul arrives at Union with God, does she remain always in Union? Yes, but not at the degree of Union which is Contact. What is the difference? It can perhaps be most easily explained (though extremely imperfectly) by referring to the union of married life. In this union, though we live in one house, we are not always both in that house at the same time; but this does not dissolve our union, and we both know our way to return there, and the right to meet is always ours. When we are both in the house, although not in the same room, there is a much nearer feeling about it, and we are apt to give a momentary call one to the other, just to have the pleasure of response: yet, though we are aware the other one is in the house and that there is no part of the house where we are forbidden to meet—it is not enough; love requires more: it will be necessary for one to go and seek the actual presence of the other (the soul does this by a quiet prayer with perhaps a few words, but more probably no words). The one finds the other one; but the other one is occupied, so the one waits patiently (this is passive contemplation), and suddenly the occupied one is so constrained by love for the waiting one that he must turn to her, open wide his arms, and embrace her—they meet, they touch, they are content.

In spiritual life this is contact or ecstasy or rapture. Here comes in the immensity of the difference between joys physical and joys spiritual—physical joys being limited to five senses: spiritual joys being above senses and open to limitless variations; but in order that these may be known in their fullness, we must eventually (after leaving the flesh) rise to immense heights of perfection: the joys enjoyed by the Archangel would *destroy* a lesser angel: the degree of joy that invigorates the saint, that sends him into rhapsodies of happiness, would *destroy* the sinner—(becoming insupportable agony to the sinner). This celestial joy is, fundamentally, a question of the enduring of some unnameable energy. How can energy be a means of this immeasurable Divine joy? After years of experience I find I cannot go back upon the knowledge that I acquired on the very first occasion of experience—that energy *is a fundamental principle of the mystery*. But how, it may very well be asked, do sins interfere with the reception of this activity? Sins are all imperfections, thickenings of the soul from self-will: Pure soul is necessary for the *happy* reception of this celestial activity, and because impurities are automatically dissipated by this activity, and the dissipation or dispersion of them *is the most awful agony conceivable* when too suddenly done, what is bliss to the saint is the extremity of torture to the sinner.

The Immensity of God's Attraction
Now we come very fearfully and dreadfully to understand something more of the meanings, the happenings, of the Judgment Day. Christ will inflict no direct willful punishment on any soul; but when He presents Himself before all souls and they behold His Face, immediately they will receive the terrible might of the activity of celestial joy. The regenerated will endure and rejoice; the unrepentant sinner will agonize, and he must flee from before the Face of Christ because the agony that he feels is the dispersal of his imperfect soul; and where shall the sinner flee, where shall he go to find happiness? for saint and sinner alike desire happiness, and there is in Spirit-life only one happiness—the Bliss of God. So then let us be careful to prepare ourselves to be able to receive and endure this happiness, even if it can at first

be only in a small degree, so that we shall not be condemned *by our own pain* to leave the Presence of God altogether and consequently lose Celestial Pleasures; let us at least prepare ourselves to remain near enough to know something of this tremendous living. It was this Divine Activity which on the night of the Too Great Happiness so anguished my imperfect soul. But that night, and that anguish, taught my soul what she could never have learnt by any other means, and what it was I learnt I find myself unable to pass on to anyone; but that night was for my soul the turning-point of her destiny, that night altered my soul forevermore; that night I knew God as deeply as He can be known whilst the soul is in flesh.

God uses also a peculiar drawing power. All souls feeling desire towards God are to a greater or lesser degree conscious of this, and, as we know, frequently remain conscious of it as a desire and nothing further to the end of life in flesh. By means of it He draws a soul towards Himself until, because of it, the whole being is willing to make efforts at self-improvement, and this is the essential: it is this cleaning up of the character, this purification, which alone can bring us to the point where we can receive God's communications of Himself.

Ecstasies inspire and awaken the soul: they convince the mind absolutely of the existence of another form of living *and of God Himself*. The feeling for God which before ecstasy was a deep (and often very painful) longing for God now increases to a burning, never-ceasing desire for Him. Only three thoughts can be said to truly occupy a person from this stage onwards—how to please God, how to get nearer to Him, how to show practical gratitude. He may increase the flow of His Power to a soul till she is in great distress, longing to leap out of the body owing to the immensity of God's attraction. This attraction at times has a very real and sensible effect upon the body: it feels to counteract gravity, it makes the body feel so light it is about to leave the ground; it affects walking, and unaccountably changes it to staggering.

To receive this attraction can be an ecstatic condition, but is by no means ecstasy. So long as we have power to move the body by will we are not in true ecstasy. In ecstasy the body feels to be disconnected in some unaccountable manner from the will; it lies inert, though it knows itself and knows that it still lives—which fundamentally differentiates it from sleep, because in sleep we do not know our body, we do not know if we are alive or dead, we know nothing. In ecstasy is no such blankness: merely the body is perforce inert, it would be entirely forgotten but for its periods of distress. Neither can ecstasy be confused with dreaming, by even the most simple person. In dreaming, objects and events of a familiar type still surround us; the total inconsequence with which they present themselves alone makes dream-living unlike actual living, for it remains fundamentally of the same type—physical and full of persons, forms, objects, and word-thoughts. We can procure sleep by willing it, but we cannot will to procure ecstasy: we find it totally independent of will.

The Soul Becomes God's Delight

If the Divine Lover gives such joys to the soul, how does the soul give joy to the Divine Lover? Is she beautiful? She becomes so. Also the soul is a poet of the first order, though she uses no words; and the soul is a weaver of melodies, though she makes no sound; but above all, and before all, the soul is a great lover. Now we know in this earthly life that a lover desires above everything else the love of her whom he loves. Only when she whom he loves returns his love, can he truly enjoy her. So also the Divine Lover. O incomparable Love! Love gives all when it gives itself, love receives all when it receives Love. By love, then, the soul is the Delight of God.

The Form of the Soul

The soul feels to be formless; though we become aware of a *spreading* which causes her to feel of the form of a cup or a disc when she receives God, and in contemplation she feels to extend—flame-like until she meets God. She can wait for God—spread, but cannot maintain this form for long without God rejoices her by His touch. How can so formless a thing, still waiting for its Spiritual Body, be beautiful? She is beautiful because of the colors she is able to assume: she can glow with such color as no flower on earth can even faintly imitate. Celestial colors are beyond all imagination. As the soul grows in purity and is able to endure an increase of the Divine Radiations and Penetration, so she changes her colors; by her colors she delights the eye of her Maker, He touches her, she becomes yet more beautiful.

Very early in the morning God walks in His Garden of Souls, and in the evening also, and in the noonday, and in the night. The soul that knows Him knows His approach, and, preparing and adorning herself for Him—waits.

A Mystery of Love

Does God come and go? The soul feels Him there, and not there. Is she mistaken in this, and God always to be possessed, but she not dressed to receive Him? If this is so, then how grievously frequent is our failure! It is more encouraging to our own state to suppose that God lends Himself and withdraws; that He will be possessed; and He will not be. But this involves caprice. Can Perfect Love have caprice? We find that grace can be received without intermission for weeks, even months, together. Without coming and departing (although in lesser and greater intensity) the Presence of God, Love and Comfort, envelop the soul. So then we learn by our own experience that God is willing to be present amongst us continually in His Second and Third Persons.

Yet, although He is present in His Two Persons, the soul is not filled: she is unspeakably blest and happy, but not wholly satisfied till He is present to her in His First Person also. She knows immediately when He so comes, and then the Three become One, and when They become One to her, in that moment the soul enters Bliss. It is love alone which enables her to possess Him, and this love that she knows how to shed to Him is His own gift to her. So the soul cries to Him, O mystery of love, was ever such sweet graciousness as lives in thee: such exquisite felicity of giving and receiving, in which the giver and receiver in mysterious rapture of generosity are oned! And this mystery of love is not in paucity of ways, but in marvelous variety of ways and of degrees—the ways of friendship, the brother and the sister, the mother and the child, the youth and the maiden, and Thyself and we.

Love makes the soul ponder on His tastes, His will, His nature. Does He prefer even in heaven to possess Himself to Himself in His First Person? or are there parts of heaven where He is ever willing to be possessed in His fullness: where He is eternally beheld in His Three Persons by such as can endure Him? The soul believes it, and this is the goal she strives for both now and hereafter. Yet there is That of Him which is forever Alone, which will never be known or shared by the greatest of the Angels. The soul comprehends that He will have it so because of that Solitary which sits within herself, she who is made after His likeness.

Love that Forgets to Ask

For many years before coming to Union with God, I found that it had become impossible to say more than a little prayer of some five or six words, and these were said very slowly: at times I was astonished at my inability, and ashamed that these pitiful shreds were all that I could offer, and always the same thing too; I tried to vary it—I could not. When I tried to say some fine sentence, when I tried even to ask for something, I could not; it all disappeared in a feeling of such sweet love for God, and I merely said again the same old words of every day. I loved. I could do nothing more than say so, and then stay there on my knees for a little while, very near Him, fascinated, adoring. But God is not vexed with a soul when she cannot say much. Is an earthly father vexed when his child, standing there before him, forgets the words upon its lips, forgets to ask, because it loves him so? Far from it. This prayer is the commencement, the foretaste, of Contemplation.

A distinguishing mark between this prayer and Contemplation is that in even the lowest degree of Contemplation God (if one may so express the inexpressible) is Localized. Hitherto His Presence has been near—but we cannot say how near, or where, and *we cannot be sure of finding it*. After Union we are certain of finding God's Presence everywhere, and at any time. He may at times be far away, or pay no attention to us; but we know whereabouts He is, and we can go and wait outside that place where He has hidden Himself and which is no place (but a figure of speech). All this cannot be explained, but after Union God is as present to the soul in Contemplation (and far more so because of the great poignancy of it) as is a fellow-creature whom we actually see and touch, much more so because between ourself and a fellow-creature, however dear, is always a barrier: try as we may there is always a dividing line between two persons. We are two: we remain two. But when we meet God there is nothing between us and God, nothing whatever divides us, and yet we are not lost in God—that is to say, we do not disappear as a living individual consciousness, but our consciousness is increased to a prodigious degree, and we are One with God.

Spiritual Sympathy

This Oneness, in a tiny degree, can be experienced by two persons who are in close spiritual sympathy when both are simultaneously and powerfully animated by very loving thoughts of Christ, or are working together, and *giving* on account of Christ: then a fluid interchange of sympathies and interests takes place in which the barriers of individuality go down.

This same fluid interchange in a still lesser degree takes place in ordinary friendship between two friends of similar tastes; but this interchange must always be with the mental and the higher part of us, it can never take place because of the merely physical, for in the physical, dependent as it is upon senses, barriers always exist: we see this in the union of lovers—their union is merely a transitory *self*-gratification, although it may include another self in that it is mutual; but more frequently it is not even mutual, and what is a pleasure to one is at the moment distasteful to the other, though the one can easily conceal from the other that it is so, proving how complete the duality of consciousness and of feeling remains between two individuals who depend upon contiguity of *substance* (or the sense of touch) for their union, and not upon spiritual *similarity*: in spiritual similarity alone is *identity* of feeling and personality and perfect union to be found, and in this identity *deceit is impossible.*

Spiritual Self-Indulgence
The soul finds it bitterly hard to rid herself of selfishness and self-will: she gets rid of one form, only to find herself falling to another. When first my soul re-knew the Joy of God I said to myself, "I will hide it in my own bosom, I will keep it all to myself. I am become independent of all creatures, I want none of them, I cannot bear the sight or the sound of them, how joyfully I leave them all behind!—I want only my God—I want—But what is all this?—I want, I will, I, I, I, I!" Later the days come when God hides Himself from me: I can go and wait at His threshold. I may pour out all the sweetness of my love, but he makes no response; I may sing to Him all day: He will not hear; I may give Him all that I am or have, and He will not communicate Himself to me. Then I remember all the years of my striving, I remember the stress, the sweat of all that climb to His footstool—the sweat that at times was like drops of blood wrung out of the soul, out of the heart, out of the mind; and yet all forgotten in the instant of the rapture of Finding. Did He then beckon and draw and delight the soul only to madden with the anguish of more hiding and more striving: was He to be found only that He might again be lost? My soul sickened with fear, and I said, Love is a calamity; who can release me from the anguish of

it? O God, since I may no more possess Thee, grant that I may shortly pass into the dust and forever be no more, so that I may escape this pain of knowing Thy Perfections and my own necessity for Thee; and I mourned for Him till my health went.

Weeks passed, and three words came constantly to me: "Visit my sick." But I did not listen: I was sick myself with a deadly wound. Almost every day the same three words came; but I turned away resentfully from them, saying to myself, "What have the sick to do with me? I am weary of sick people: I have been so much with them. Must I accept the sick in place of the ecstasy of God? I mourn for the loss of God. I can cheer no sick." The words came again, with excessive gentleness, and the gentleness was like the gentleness of Christ, and it pierced. So that day I go to the village and visit the sick again, and I look at them tenderly and lovingly, and tenderly and lovingly they look at me, and some say, "It is as if God came into the house with you"; and tears come to my eyes, and I say, "It may be so, because He sent me," and they gaze at me lovingly, and lovingly I gaze at them; and it seems to me that I can no longer tell where "they" cease and where "I" begin, and the sweetness, the peculiar sweetness, of Christ pierces me through from my head to my feet—that sweetness that I have not known for weeks. And so I comprehend that Holy Love is not alone just Thee and me, but it is also Thee and me and the others, and Thee and the others and me.

Yet still I wanted my own way. The way I wanted was to be free in order to worship and bless God in a beautiful place, in some place that I should choose. I wanted to worship Him, and to sing Him the Song of the Soul from some quiet hill among the olive trees by the Mediterranean Sea. I wanted this marvelous, this almost terrible, joy of meeting God in a beautiful place that I should choose: I wanted it so that it became spiritual greed—spiritual self-indulgence.

Duty, heavy-winged duty, prevented my taking the journey; duty to an always-contrary relation, now unwell. It was only a little thing just a journey prevented, but it crossed my self-will; and in an impatient, detestable way that I have, I wanted to push all duty, even all human relationships, anywhere upon one side, or over the edge of the world, so they might all fall together out of my sight and I be free! Because I thought these thoughts, I came to the Place of Tribulation. And the Messenger came, and he said, "Escape, and the way is consenting." But I said, "No, I will not have that way, I will escape by some other way." So I tried every other way, but found it guarded by something which seemed to be armed with a hammer; but I persisted: then for days and nights my soul stood up to the hammers and received terrible blows, and still I persisted—I would find a way to escape that should please my will. But I could not eat, I could not sleep, the flesh visibly lessened on my bones, and at last I loathed myself and my own will and my own soul, and I cried to God, "Shall I never be through with this terrible struggle with self-will?" and groaned aloud in my despair. Then the words that were sent long ago to a saint, and that he was inspired to write down to help us all, now came and did their work for me through him: "My grace is sufficient for thee." And so I found it, and more than sufficient—when I consented.

Who is it, what is it, that so punishes the soul? Is it God? No. Patiently, lovingly He waits. Our pain is the difficulty of consenting to perfection: every virtue has a hammer, every perfection a long two-edged sword; and the punishment we feel is the breaking and wounding of self-will under the hammers of the virtues and the sword-thrusts of the vision of perfection. Put aside these wretched, these sometimes awful and terrible, battles and punishments, shrink from them when they come, and we may put aside salvation. Accept them—stand up to the hammer and take the blows and learn: consent to the sword that pierces up to the hilt, and what do we come to?—The Blisses of God.

CHAPTER 4
The God-Force of Love

The Sweetest of Prayers

After coming to Union with God, our prayers become entirely changed, not only in the manner of presenting them, but changed also in what is presented. Petitioning is a hard thing. I had found it easy to pray for others whether I loved them or not, with the lips and with some of the heart; but I found that I could not do it in the new way, with all my heart, mind, soul, and strength, so that everything else fled away into nothing and was no more, except that for which I petitioned God. A perfect concentration for the welfare of a stranger or of some cause was a very hard thing; yet I was made aware that I must learn to do it.

For two or three years I suffered pain and exhaustion over this petitioning; I would be so fatigued by it, found it so great a strain, that I said to myself, "I shall lose my health over this petitioning, for as I do it, it is as though I gave my life-energy for the cause or person for whom I pray." But my Good Angel whispered me not to give in, but continue to be willing, continue to be generous, no matter the cost. I am not generous, but I went on with it, and secretly had the greatest dread of it; my whole nature shrank from the effort, from the strange loss of vitality this petitioning brought. Then at last, after more than two years, because of remaining willing, because of trying to remain generous about this, to me, most grievously hard prayer, one happy day God lifted away all the strain and difficulty, all the pain and fatigue, and turned it into the sweetest of prayers: into a new song, a new honey, new music, a new delight, in which the soul has, as it were, but to sip at the nectar of His Love and Beneficence, to bring it to a fellow-soul.

I found that God causes the soul to pray this joyous, this exquisite, prayer for total strangers, passers-by in the street, fellow-travelers by road and rail, here and there, this one and that, she knows which one it is: how surprised these persons would be if they knew that a total stranger, who never saw them before and never will see them again, was joyously, lovingly, holding them up before God for His help and

51

His blessing! and they receive His blessing. God does not prompt such prayers for nothing. Is this favoritism? No; they are secretly seeking Him.

To Think Continually of God

When the soul is united to God a great change comes over the mind, which now thinks continually, lovingly, of God—God not merely hoped for, looked for, as in the past, but God found and known, God close and near. What are amongst the most noticeable changes in the mind? First, we notice it has become very simple in its requirements, and very restful; it no longer darts here and there gathering in this and that of fancied treasures, as a bird darts at flies; it has dropped outside objects, in order to hover around thoughts of God, which at the same time are not particularized, but, as it were, quietly, contentedly, float in a general and peaceful fragrance of beauty.

Ordinarily the mind would find it difficult to hover in this way with such a singleness of intent, but in certain other cases we see the same contentment—in the mother beside her babe: though she may not talk to it, or touch it, she is happy; she knows it near, she is secretly giving to it. We see it in the babe also: it gazes at its mother and is quiet; if the mother removes herself, the child may cry; no one has hurt it—merely, it has ceased to be happy because the object of its desire has gone too far from it, has disappeared. We see it also in two lovers; they sit near together, and the more they love the fewer words they require to speak. Separate them, and they spend their time uneasily in sending messages, in thinking numberless yearning thoughts which become painful, and, if continued for long, can affect the health. Put them together again, and they barely say two words: their joy at meeting occupies the whole of their attention. It is the same when we love God. The heart, and the mind, and the soul are blissfully content, they are in a love-state, they bask in His Presence.

Awareness of God

Does God, then, when experienced feel to be a Fire? Yes, and no, for we feel that we shall be consumed, and yet it is not burning but a blissful energy of the most inexpressible and unbearable intensity, which has the feeling of disintegrating or *dispersing* flesh. The experience is blissful to heart and mind only so long as it is given within certain limits: beyond this it is bliss-agony, beyond this it would soon be death to the body; and the soul feels that in her imperfect state it can soon easily be the dispersion of herself also. How, then, can it be possible that God can take up His abode with us and we still live? In all contacts with God we notice one fact pre-eminently—they do not take place with the mind, but with that which was previously unknown to us, and which communicates the joy and the realities of meeting God to the mind. What is this? It does not live in the heart: it lives, or feels to live, in the upper cavity of the chest, above the heart, and below the throat-base. It can endure God. It is spirit, it feels to be a higher part of the soul: we might call it the Intelligence and Will of the soul, because it acts for the soul as the mind acts for the body, it is above the soul as the mind is above (more important than) and rules an arm or leg. The more we experience God, the more we are forced to comprehend that we have in us an especial organ in this spirit with which we can communicate with God and by which we can receive Him without the mind or body being destroyed. For when God takes up His abode with a man He will communicate Himself to this loving Spirit-Will or Intelligence in ecstasies. And through His Son He will communicate Himself in another manner, to the heart and mind, so graciously, with such a tender care, that without the stress of ecstasy we are kept in a delicate and most blessed Awareness of God. In these ways we can know, even in flesh, the beginnings of the true love-state, the beginnings of the angelic state, which is this same love-state brought *to completion by Beholding God.*

Although this blessed condition of Awareness of God is a gift, and at first the mind and soul are maintained in it without effort on their part, it being accomplished for them solely by the power of the Grace of God, yet later—and somewhat to their dismay after receiving such favors—they discover that it must be worked for in order to be maintained. The heart must give, the mind must give, the soul must give: when they neither work nor give they may find themselves receiving nothing: God ceases to be present to them. Generosity on our part is required. It works out in experience to be always the same thing that is needed for our perfect health and happiness—reciprocity. Without we maintain this reciprocity we shall experience *extraordinary disappointment.*

Real Education

We hope for much from "education"; but what education is it that will be of enduring value to us? Is it the education which teaches us the grammars of foreign languages, scientific facts, the dates when wars were won, when kings ascended their thrones, princes died, artists painted their masterpieces, that will bring us to our finest opportunities of success? To the soul there is little greater or less chance of success offered by the degree of "polish" in the education we have the money to procure: the peasant who cannot read or write may achieve the purpose of life before the savant: we know it without caring to acknowledge it to ourselves: the education that we really require is the education of daily conduct, the education of character, the education by which we say to Self-will, to Pride, and to Lusts, "Lie down!"—and they do it! When a soul knows herself, has repented and become redeemed, she knows all other souls, good or bad: there are no longer any secrets for her, no one can hide himself from her: she sees all these open and living books, reads them, and avoids judging and bitterness in spite of the selfishness, stupidity, and frailty revealed on every page: she finds the same faults in herself; selfishness, stupidity, and weakness are engraved upon herself; the redeemed and enlightened soul with tears perpetually corrects these faults: the unenlightened soul does not—this is the difference between them.

Hand Your Trials Over to God

For some time after coming to Union with God we remain convinced that all now being so well with the soul all will be well with the body also, and the health does improve and become more stable; but the day comes when we learn that God is not concerned with saving flesh, and that the body must share the usual fate—we shall continue to suffer through it. But we also discover that there can be a marvelous amelioration to this suffering. By raising the consciousness to its highest—that is to say, by living with the highest part of the soul *and waiting upon God*—we can experience such very great Grace that the poignancy, the distress, of pain disappears.

For instance, the following is from my experience. Trouble has come, trouble of several kinds: the death of one very dear; severe illness to another; for my brother a serious operation; for myself a slight one, but a very painful one—in fine, a variety of trials all coming together as they have a way of doing. I feel terribly nervous and fearful of the pain of my own operation and my brother's also; he is the brother who once saved my life, he is the being who more than anyone on earth I have most loved since early childhood. So I hang on to God. I hang to Him, not by beseeching Him to relieve or release me from any of these inevitable happenings, but by the way I have so slowly been learning, in which a creature, by means and because of love, passes out of itself and is able to hand over to God everything which it is or has or thinks or does, and in exchange receives His Peace.

So I hand over my brother and my dead and my anxieties for self into His hands, and I go to my operation with the same serenity that I should go to meet a friend. I notice that I am more calm, less nervous, than anyone else. The anesthetic fails before the operation is completed: consciousness returns and becomes aware of atrocious pain and blood-soaked busy instruments. Yet by Grace of God the mind and soul are able immediately to raise and maintain themselves in high consciousness of God, and the operation can be finished without a cry or movement of the body. And this Grace is continued for days afterwards, so that in recalling the torturing incidents, and though the pain of wounds continues severe enough to interfere with sleep, yet my mind remains quite calm, like a quiet lake over which, without ruffling its waters, hangs a mist—a tranquil shroud of pain that has no sting, no fear, no fret.

Suffering Only Can Cleanse

After coming to Union with God I *never lacked anything*, and this during the most difficult times of the war, and under every and all circumstances. Being careful to try and observe how this was worked, I saw it was very naturally and simply done by everyone being given an impulse to help me, always without any request to them on my part: the porter, besieged by twenty persons, would be blind to all and, coming straight to me, would offer his service; the taxi-driver, hailed by a waiting mob, had eyes and ears for no one but myself, yet I had made him no sign except by looking at him. I never lacked anything for one hour: *but I continually asked Christ to help me.* Since coming to Union with God, I have had innumerable trials, some of them tortures, but have been brought safely out of every one. I afterwards found that each trial was exactly what was needed for the alteration of some objectionable characteristic in myself. No trial that came was unnecessary. When its work was accomplished, the trial disappeared.

Can it be said that Union with God in this world entails upon us increased sufferings here? Yes. But these sufferings are not owing to abnormal occurrences: nothing will happen which is not the common lot of humanity; merely we are caused to feel that which we do experience, very acutely; and after Union with God all earthly consolations must be abandoned: until we abandon these we do not know how we have depended on them, how they have protected us from depression, loneliness, boredom, and discontent. Abandon all these earthly consolations and interests, and at the same time *be abandoned by God* (sensible Grace is withdrawn), and immediately our sufferings become very severe, though our outward circumstances may appear, and may actually remain, of the very best. If our house is a fine one, we must live in it completely, detached from its attractions: the same with regard to our friends, our amusements, our wealth, and all our possessions. It is obvious that in learning to do this we shall often suffer. The soul has painfully to learn that without God's Grace there is no virtue, no righteousness, and no sanctity: she learns by going forward upon Grace—perhaps to some great height: then Grace is withdrawn, the soul falls back, and feels to fall lower than she ever was before, and usually she falls over a trifle. Amazed, unspeakably surprised and humiliated, and ashamed, the soul learns to know herself—to know herself with God, to know herself without God. When she is with God, there seems no height to which she cannot rise: this gives great courage: more and more she abandons everything distasteful to God in order to unite herself more securely to Him.

We have no sufferings that are not useful to us. Looking back on my life, I see how many troubles I suffered: how often my health suffered (malaria and sun fevers, and lightning and its consequences): how I was and still am kept in a somewhat fragile state of health, though quite free of all actual disease. I see in this frailness, especially during the earlier years of my life, an immense protection: given full and vigorous health, combined with my selfish and passionate temperament, and I know very well I should have fallen in any and all kinds of dangers at all times. I was not to be trusted with robust health, and even after all the mercies and blessings God has showered upon me I do not trust myself. I still remain the sinner, fundamentally and potentially at every step the sinner. But Love and Grace surround the sinner. Love and Grace save the sinner from himself: Love and Grace can beautify and make the sinner shine.

My physical sufferings are not to be compared with the sufferings I see others endure, and endure cheerfully: this is a great shame and humiliation to me, because I have not learnt to suffer cheerfully: I am too easily undone by suffering and by the sight of suffering in any living thing; but although one may be a coward—that is to say, one may inwardly shrink from every kind of suffering—one can be, and it is necessary to be, quite submissive; and to refrain from the slightest rebellion or selfishness—this is what God takes note of. There is nothing but suffering that can cleanse us, nothing but pain and misfortune which can so thoroughly convince us of our own nothingness, and break self-pride: joy will not do it; joy can do nothing more than refresh us after our sufferings, and in almost all lives we see how joy is made to alternate with sorrow: it encourages, it stimulates to further endeavors (this is the reason that God, at a certain stage of progress, gives extraordinary blisses, ecstasies, and so on), but it does not disperse our blemishes: the dispersal of spiritual blemishes is, as we know, the main reason of life in the flesh; it must be done, and the sooner the better: then we can finish, once and for all, with flesh existence.

Righteous and very virtuous people may be able to dispense with Divine joys and consolations: it is doubtful if many sinners can—they require the confidence, the certainty, the enthusiasm which is naturally kindled by such experiences. So then we find that the vicissitudes of life, the endless daily trials, do not go because we find God. But His Grace comes, and when His Grace is with us, wet or shine is all one, love and beauty gently sparkle everywhere; and then, the heart cries out to him: Every day is like a jewel, every day I see the whole world decked and garlanded with all; the beauty of Thy mind: each tree, each flower, each bee or bird tremulous with the life and wonder of Thy creative ingenuity! Each day is a new jewel set upon the necklace of my thoughts of Thee.

On Trials
One of the trials that we have to endure as beginners is a joyless, flat, ungracious condition; a kind of paralysis of the soul, a dreary torpor. When we would approach God—pray to Him—He is nowhere to be found: He has disappeared, and everything to do with finding Him is become hard work, such hard work that it suddenly seems to us quite unprofitable: we suddenly remember a number of outside things

which we would far sooner do: we try to pray, but the prayer goes nowhere-in-particular; it has no enthusiasm, no force behind it: has prayer then suddenly re-become a duty? This is terrible; what shall we do—shall we ask God to help us? When we do, we do it in so half-hearted a manner that our prayer feels to merely float around our own head like some miserable mist. We feel certain that this joyless, withered state will endure to the end of life on earth (the conviction that our unhappy condition is permanent is characteristic of all severe trials, because if we supposed the condition or difficulty only momentary it would not produce a sufficient trial, and consequent effort to overcome it on our part). This trial (though it may not always be a trial, but an actual blemish of the soul, a serious lack of unselfish love which must at once be strenuously corrected) is given for several reasons—we have become, perhaps, too greedy of *enjoyment* of prayer: or we have come to take this joyousness of prayer for granted: or we have come to think we are uncommonly clever at knowing how to love and to pray; that we know so well how to do it that we can do it of our own power and capacity without God's assistance. Or the trial may be sent not for any of these reasons, but solely in order to increase the strength and perseverance of our love to God, and of our Generosity.

This is one trial, and another is that God allows us to become convinced that He has nothing more to give us, He withdraws His graciousness from our apprehension; He leaves us as a tiny, unwanted, meaningless speck, alone in a vast universe. It would be idle to say that the soul does not suffer from this change; but these sufferings are just what she requires in order to develop courage, humility, endurance, love, and generosity. These two trials—the one when love is all dried up on our part, and the other when we think love must be all dried up on God's part—are the finest possible training and exercise for the soul, but they are only such if the soul *tries ardently to overcome them*: it is in the effort to overcome that virtue is learnt, progress made. There is one most splendid remedy. Is it asking of God? No, it is giving to God. We give Him thanks and we bless Him, and we tell Him that we love Him, and we do it with all our heart, mind, soul, and strength, and this becomes possible even though a moment ago we were so far from Him, so tepid, seemingly so estranged: it becomes possible because we remember all the wonderful things that God has done for us and given us, and made for us, and suffered for us; and in remembering these it is impossible but that love and gratitude, like a torch of enthusiasm, will presently flare up in us.

The Higher Part of the Soul
The heart, mind, soul, and will work together and lead together the reasonable earthly existence; but there is another part of the soul, a higher part, which has its own intelligence, which leads no earthly existence, has no direct recognition of *material being;* thinks no earth-thoughts, judges by no man-made standards, sins no earth-sins. Has this part of the soul, then, never sinned? *It feels* that it has sinned, though it cannot say how or when, but it *feels* that this sin was direct as between itself and God, and is the cause of its separation from God; and it feels this sin to have been *an infidelity.* It is with this part of the soul that we sin the unforgivable sin against the Holy Ghost, which cannot be sinned by mere natural man: (here we touch the mystery of the two orders of sinning which, to the initiated, are seen both to be covered by the same commandments). This higher part of the soul mourns and longs for God with a terrible longing, and can be consoled, satisfied, by God only; He communicates Himself to this part of the soul. Sins of heart and mind do not injure it, but retard it: it cannot be corrupted by material living, because it does not connect itself directly with earth-living, it "responds" to God alone; but earthly sins delay it, paralyze its powers, postpone indefinitely its return to God. Is it this part of the soul which we ordinarily speak of as the Will? It cannot be, since it is with our Will that we consent to earth-sins. Have we, then, two Wills? It is reasonable and it conforms with experience to say that we have two Wills—a Spirit-Will conducting Spirit-living, and a Reasoning or Mind-Will, conducting the affairs of earth-living: the lower part of the soul is the meeting-place and the intermediary between these two (often opposing) Wills, it is the ground upon which they work and have their fruitions.

The Spirit-Will is the Will by which we finally become united to God. Before regeneration we are unaware in any keen degree of its existence; but it may exist for us in a vague and confused manner as an incomprehensible, undefined yearning: we cannot satisfy this yearning, because we do not know what it requires for its satisfaction. It is above conscience: conscience has its seat in the lower soul, there it deals with the affairs of earthly life. This Spirit-Will is so far above conscience (which can be used, cultivated, improved, or destroyed, according to our own desire) that it is not given into the keeping or cognizance of the "natural" man, but remains unknown, inoperative until re-awakened and impregnated with renewed vigor by direct Act of God in the regenerated man. This awakening, this reinvigoration, would seem to be synonymous with the Baptism of the Holy Ghost.

If it is awakened only by Act of God, in what way can we be held responsible about it? Our responsibility, our part, our opportunity is to so order the lower or earth-will that God shall see us to be prepared for the awakening of the Spirit-Will. This Spirit-Will, once awakened, is never again shut out from direct communication with God. Even when Grace is withdrawn, this Will-Spirit can come before God and, no barrier between, know Him *there*; although He may deny it all consolation and leave it languishing, it yet retains the consolation of its one supreme necessity—that of knowing *it has not lost Him*. It waits.

Aspire to the Perfect
Like knows like: it does not "know" its opposite, but is drawn towards its opposite before and without "knowing" it: here we have the cause of the condescension of the Good towards the imperfect, and of the aspiration of the imperfect to the perfect long before it can "know" the perfect. Without this attraction of like to opposite the imperfect could not become the perfect (we desire, are drawn to God, long before we are able to know Him). The imperfect is able to become the perfect by continually aspiring to it: it gradually becomes "like." There are no barriers in spirit-living, therefore there is nothing to prevent the soul becoming perfect, save its own will-failure. The barrier existing between physical-living and spirit-living can only be overcome in and by a man's own soul: in the soul these two forms of living can meet and become known by the one individual, who can live alternately in the two modes, but it is necessary that the will and preference shall be continually given and bent towards spiritual-living, physical-living being accepted patiently and as a cross. Then flesh ceases to be a barrier to spiritual living. This is the work of Christ and of the Holy Ghost. Because the soul has recaptured the knowledge of this rapturous living we are not to suppose that it is possible to continually enjoy it here or introduce its glories into social and worldly living: it is between the soul and God only; but earth-life can and should by this knowledge be entirely readjusted.

Is This World Real?

Are we correct in saying or supposing that this world with all that we see in it (because perishable) is not real, and that the Invisible is the only Real? We are using the wrong word: all that we see here is real after its own manner: it is intentional, it is designed, it is magnificent, it is the evidence in fixed form of the Supreme Intelligence; how can we venture to call it unreal, nothing, negligible? It is a question not of Reality or Unreality, but of greater and of lesser Activity. In this world we see the Divine Energy slowed down to its least degree: we see it so much slowed down that the Divine Ideas can become crystallized into a form and for their decreed period remain fixed. It is exactly this which the soul requires in order to recover her lost bearings. She needs the Beautiful, the Good, and, the Bad made sensible to her in *fixed objects*, and Time in which to consider them and make her choice between them.

When Spirit-living is experienced, we become aware that in spirit-life Activity is of such an order as to preclude the mode of it being in fixed forms and objects: so there is no fixed visible Beauty, no fixed visible Good or Bad, no fixed *results*, and the soul "sees" and "knows" only *that which she herself is like to*. If she is bad, she cannot become better by the privilege of looking at that which is good. If she thinks or desires wrong, she remains wrong: she must think Right in order to produce or "know" Right. She loses God because she can no longer think godly, and nothing is fixed by which she can trace Him: it is like to like, and this instantaneously without pause (or time). Here in this world Like may behold its Opposite: Bad may behold Good and, because of being able to behold it, may go over and join its will to Good: it is able to do this because the evidence of Good remains fixed whether the beholder or thinker is good or bad.

As in free spirit we think a thought and become it, have a desire flash to it and are it, it is easy to see how in thinking thoughts that are not godly, desiring that which is ungodly and imperfect, we pass far from God by "becoming" imperfection; and, having "become," find no satisfaction, satisfaction resting with God only. Having ceased to think godly, the soul loses God, becomes insensitive, and falls into darkness, thinks of her own wretchedness and, thinking of it, is held fast to it. Being miserable, she thinks to Self; thinking of Self, she is bound to the solitude of Self—blank solitude without fixed objects to amuse, without fixed Beauty to lead higher, to restore, to calm. Is all this tantamount to saying that when separated from God, Spirit-life is less desirable than earth-life? It is: for then we are "dead" to celestial-living, and in Spirit-life all other living is miserable living. Hence we see the dire necessity of the soul for a Savior: the necessity of fixed forms, of time, of flesh (which is a fixed stay-point for the soul), of the Incarnation of the Savior *in flesh* in order that He may guide the soul amongst these fixed forms, Himself showing her which to choose and which to cast aside: we see the necessity of time in order that, though we have an ungodly thought, we have *time* to repent and choose a better before, in a horrible rapidity, we are inevitably *become that which we had thought.*

In this world, this stay-point for the soul, the most lost is enabled to enjoy and perceive Beauty and Goodness. How much more easy, then, to return to godly thoughts, to the Good, to God Himself! But though her Savior is in this world so near to the soul, she does not always seek Him. He belongs to the Invisible. Intoxicated at finding herself amused amongst fixed objects which she enjoys lazily through fixed mediums of the five senses, she devotes herself to these objects, surrounds herself with them, forgets everything else. "It is harder for the rich man to enter the kingdom of heaven." But she must abandon object-worship: this is not to say she is to deny the existence of objects, calling them unreal; she must despise no created object, for each is there to form for her an object-lesson. She has two choices: she can see the objects, remain satisfied with them, and seek no further. Or, she can see the objects, admire them, but seek beyond them for their Instigator and Creator. Now she is on the track of God. All is well.

Happiness at Lightning Velocity

The way of return to God is the same way by which we came out from Him—reversed. We came away by means of greeds and curiosities imagined by Self-will. The return is by casting away these greeds, casting away all prides, all selfishness; and what self-loving soul is there that could or would, left alone to herself, conceive of following such a way of cruel necessities, of such hard endurance without an Example before her? For the way is a hard way, a toiling way, at times an awful way, and as we pursue it the burden grows heavier, the pain sharper: then it grows lighter as the soul becomes renewed; and the pain is no longer the pain of loneliness, of sin and sorrow, but becomes the pain of Love, waiting in certainty for an ultimate Reunion: it becomes pain which is being forgotten in the returning happiness of God.

But first must come the abandonment of Self-will, bit by bit, to the death. So we see upon the Cross, Christ stripped of everything, and at the last stripped even of Union with the Father: consenting to bear the pains of even Spiritual Death: "My God, my God, why hast Thou forsaken Me?" If there could be any greater depth of pain, He would have shared that also with the wandering soul. So we are indeed one with Him in everything: and He with us.

In Spirit-life we meet the Ideas of God un-crystallized into any form. They penetrate the soul—she flashes to them, she becomes them, she reaches unimaginable heights of bliss by "becoming." This form of joy is incomprehensible until experienced: it is stupendous living, if it may be so expressed it is happiness at lightning velocity; but it is a lightning happiness which must flash to God. When it ceases to do this in a full manner, it ceases to be full happiness.

The soul longs for happiness; feels certain she was created for it. So she is. Looking at the masses of drab, ugly, and unsuccessful lives around us, we may well ask what purpose and what progress is there in the lives of all these hopeless-looking people. But there is not one life that does not have brought before it, and into it, the opportunity of, and the invitation to, self-sacrifice, and in a greater or lesser degree this is accepted and responded to by all. There is far more soul-progress made by these gray-looking lives than would appear on the surface: they accept self-sacrifice—they accept Duty—all is well. Very much progress may not be made during the one earth-period of life, but some is made: we drifted away slowly from God; our return is slow.

The God-Force of Love

Love is not the mere pleasant sentiment of the heart we are apt to consider it: it is *the animating principle of the soul*, it is the reason and cause of her existence: it is a God-Force. When a soul does not love God she has ceased to respond to this Force; she is no longer a "sensitive" or *living* soul: when she becomes insensitive, she has become what flesh is when it is "callous."

This insensitiveness is the one great predominating disease of the soul: it is the cause of the darkness in which the soul finds herself in this world: it is this which causes our unawareness of God and of Celestial-living. How can we commence to remedy this disastrous state? We can act nobly, we can be generous, doing what we do as though it were for love, although it is merely Duty which animates us. This will be more or less joyless, because love alone can make acts joyful; but though it may be joyless it will advance the soul immensely: it will advance her to the highest degrees required by God in order that He shall Retouch her. When He Retouches her she becomes reanimated, she once again commences to live for and because of love: she becomes "sensitive" to God. This Retouching may occur only after the soul is free of the body—but the body is the house which our examination must be passed in which we must prepare and qualify for this Retouching. Hence the importance of continuing to make every effort *in this life*. The soul which takes Christ into herself, loves Him, obeys Him, tries to copy Him, qualifies fully for this Retouching.

Sorrow Is to Melt the Heart

In early youth life may be, and often is, a joyous adventure: little by little we grow aghast at the amount of suffering which life really stands for—our own sufferings and those of others, of which, owing to our own pains, we gradually take more and more note. Why all this suffering? It appalls, it frightens, it makes upon many hearts and minds a sinister impression: how is this suffering of innocents to be reconciled with the Benign Will of a God Who is Perfect Love? Let us cease thinking that indiscriminate suffering to creatures is the Will of God. What is it, then? It is the inevitable—the long drawn-out sequence to the soul's departure from God—the Source of Happiness.

The beginning of Salvation is to think. Nothing causes us to think so much as sorrow, suffering, and pain; and they melt the heart also, and they humble pride. The man who has never suffered, and never loved, is more to be pitied than the paralytic: his chance of Life is remote.

How can we reasonably expect that the road back to our long-since forsaken God is to be smooth, pleasant, velvet-covered. What divides us from God? Is it happiness, beauty, and light? No—self-indulgence, rocks of evil, ugly greeds, places of sin and selfishness. Can we climb back through all this, most of it in darkness, without tears, without pain, without every kind of anguish? Over this part of the road is no peace; but continue, and, little by little, peace comes.

We say that we must find Christ; but where, and how, shall we find this Mighty Lord, Who comes out from the Father to meet the Prodigal? Must we study in ecclesiastical colleges, travel to distant lands, visit holy places, kneel on celebrated sacred ground, kiss stones, attend ceremonies, look at bones? No! Stand still! Just where we are is the place where we can meet Him. Just where we stand today can be as sacred, as blessed, as the Holy Land. Some little wood sprinkled with flowers, our own quiet room, an unknown, nameless hillside— these can be as holy as Mount Carmel, because He meets us there.

A Faculty Above Reason

It may well be asked of a soul which claims to have found God, How does she know that she has encountered Him? We have a Critical Faculty. It is above Reason, because it sifts and judges the findings of Reason, throwing out or retaining what Reason has deduced. This is a Higher-Soul faculty: it concerns itself solely with knowing Perfection. Reason is not occupied with knowing Perfection, but in analyzing and digesting all alike that is brought to it.

It is to the Critical Faculty that art, poetry, and music appeal, and make their thought-suggestions. We do not enjoy music because of the noise, but because of the thoughts suggested by it—we float upon these emotion-thoughts (we may float low, we may float high, and do not know to where; but it is somewhere where we cannot get without the music), so we say we love the music; but it is the emotion-thoughts we love. The sound and the thoughts suggested by it appeal to the Critical Faculty of the Soul, and, if it is perfect enough to be accepted by this faculty, we may pass, for the time being, into soul-living, but only very delicately, tentatively, and nothing to be compared to the soul-living produced by the Touch of God.

When God communicates Himself to the soul, she lives in a manner never previously conceived of, reaching an experience of living in which every perfection is present to her as Being there in such unlimited abundance that the soul is overwhelmed by it and must fall back to less, because of insupportable excess of Perfections. This perfection of living is given, and is withdrawn, outside of her own will. Which is the more sane and reasonable—for the soul to think, I have invented and originated a new and *perfectly satisfying* form of living; or for the soul to conclude that she has been admitted to the re-encounter of perfect—or Celestial—living? In this living are happenings which cannot be communicated, or even indicated to others, because they reach beyond words, beyond all or any other experience, beyond any possible previous imagination or expression of mind, beyond all particularization; it is these occasions of experience which the Critical Faculty regards as being encounters with the Supreme Spirit, because they are complete; nothing is wanting; they afford life at its perfection point—a stupendous Felicity, and that *Repose* in bliss for which all souls secretly long. It is the meeting of the Wisher with the Wished; of Desire with the Desired: and yet, being that which it is—unthinkable Fulfillment—it is above all, or any, Wishes, and beyond Desire; it can be known, but not named.

In High Contemplation we find that if Reason attempts activity, nothing is consummated: she must submerge herself and wait: soon Reason discovers the wherefore of this—her activity is not the activity of That Other. Only by that which is like in activity can That Other be received: this "like" is not herself: finally she comes to know this "like" as a higher part of the soul—Spirit. When Spirit has received and given it to the soul, then it is afterwards the part of Reason to attack from every side that which has been received, to digest it, absorb it, and share it, in fact though not in act. According to the health and strength of Reason so we shall successfully deal with and use that with which the Spirit presents us. By comparison with the magnificent Spirit-Activity or Spirit-Intelligence the Reason is limited and frail as a new-born babe: this is no humiliation to Reason, since she should not be expected to accomplish that which is not her part.

The Ecstasy of Contact

Why do not all men apprehend God? It is very questionable if all men desire to do so, because in the recesses of each man's soul lies the consciousness that there will be some great price to pay. But beyond this there arises the question: Is it a desirable price or no price, that all souls should come while still in flesh to immediate knowledge of, and contact with, God; and after long and close thinking the experienced soul will answer No, and Yes. No, in so far as the apprehension of the Godhead is concerned; Yes, and most vitally Yes, for Christians, in so far as Communion and Contact with Christ is concerned. Why this distinction? Because the apprehension of the Godhead is beyond the requirements of salvation and redemption, and the world and flesh were created for those purposes. Though there is no limit to the heights to which the soul may aspire, and all souls are invited eventually to behold the Face of God, if so be they shall be able to prepare themselves to endure Him, there are to a soul still in flesh the most terrible dangers in knowing the Fullness of God even so far as His Fullness may be Known to Flesh in an acute degree over a period of many years and can never be said to cease altogether.

The Soul knows and feels, when in its acute stage, this horrible danger without comprehending its exact cause and nature, but it has about it the feeling that a man might have standing balanced on a narrow pinnacle. Unapproachable, untouchable only so long as he remains upon the summit, the eyes of a thousand enemies watch for his smallest descent: they watch day and night. What alone can enable the Soul to maintain such a position? Hourly, often momently, Communion with Jesus Christ. What makes such perseverance likely or even possible on the soul's part? Only love can make it so.

If we say Communion with Christ is for the Christian vital to a full redemption, and therefore the Apprehension of Him is essential, to what degree should we experience this Apprehension of Him? The degree at which, perceiving in Him and His ways our Ideal, we become willing to modify and change *our manner of thinking and doing* in order to meet the requirements of this Ideal. Having gone so far, the soul is likely to become enamored of Him Personally: then all is indeed well for her.

So then we find that we can apprehend God by an ever-ascending scale of degrees. We can apprehend Him with the Reason and the heart at all hours of the day. We can seek and approach Him with the holy white passion of the Mind. Yet this is not the Apprehension of Him which alone can be termed Contact, and which alone satisfies the soul or gives us the full feeling that we Know God. We cannot "Know" God as fully as He can be known by flesh without we enter ecstasy; but it is not ecstasy which produces the meeting with God, but the meeting with God which produces the ecstasy. And when He comes the Reason does not receive Him, but that certain small part, little more than a point in the soul receives Him.

Apart from the joy of it, what is the true value of ecstasy to him to whom it is granted? It raises him above Faith into Certitude. The peace and strength given by Certitude are such that Joy is neither here nor there, the soul can wait for it, because, no matter what may afterwards happen to such a one, he remembers, and remains once and for all aware, that God Is, *and that He can be Known*: he learns also a new knowledge, but cares nothing for this because it is knowledge or because it is power, but because it brings him nearer to his God.

The Soul's Caprice

Life in this world is a life for spiritual weaklings. Our eternal Self is an Intelligence, a Desire, and a Will, and the life we live with it is no idle, torpid, confined living such as we have here, but is a living *in Liberty*, without limit, restriction, fatigue, or satiety; in it word thoughts and thinking are superseded; by comparison to it even the highest thought-achievements of men, their noblest aspirations, appear like the sand-castles of children. Ravished at such further revelations of the Genius of God, the soul at last knows satisfaction. It requires perfection in order to be permanently operative, because only in perfection is Freedom found, and because for the living of it nothing can remain but such Essentials of the soul *as cannot be dispersed*. It is a measureless Generosity and an ecstasy of Receiving and Giving. To say that purity and perfection are required for this living is no mere arbitrary dictum, but a scientific fact: the impure, imperfect soul finds herself unable in, perfect liberty and freedom, *to expand to interaction* with the Divine Activity. When the process of Return is sufficiently completed and, being still in flesh, we enter for a brief time this living, Reason, Pain and Evil, Yesterday, and Tomorrow disappear. Reason is gathered up into, and superseded by, the spiritual and wordless Intelligence: Pain and Evil, their part and work accomplished, are dispersed and banished into the mists of darkness.

So the soul may learn even from this world something of the mystery of the Depths of God. She may enter into the happiness of Union with the Three in One: the One Whom in a state of glory yet to come she may Behold. But beyond This of Him which He will allow her to Behold, beyond This of Him in which she may repose in bliss, and beyond this Repose which He wills her to know of Him, He shows her that yet more of Him Is which He will share—heights of Felicity beyond all measure, holding the soul till she must pray Him to release her, or she will perish—reeling depths of rapture in a mystery of light; bliss beyond bliss for that lover who shall venture—all Eternity unfolding in fulfillment.

And yet remains That of Him which wills no reciprocity, but shares Himself with Himself. So peace Is. And so, even in not giving,

He yet does give that which is most precious, for without He Himself in His forever hidden depths were Peace, His creatures could neither know nor have peace.

Looking into herself, what does the soul perceive? Apart from sins and virtues she perceives two things—caprice and free-will. Neither are of her own creation, but are essentials of her being. It may be that in caprice and free-will she may find an answer to those two questions which stir her to her depths: What is she that God should so love her? and how she to be away from Him? Clothed in the body of either man or woman, the soul is predominantly feminine—the Feminine Principle beloved of, and returning to, the Eternal Masculine of God. Caprice is feminine; Caprice and Mystery are two enchanting sisters, and in Woman we see them as being irresistible to Man. Angels, though they are a glory of God's heaven, cannot alone satisfy all the needs of their Creator: they have neither sex nor caprice, nor the mystery which joins hands with it. So He creates the soul, and He gives her an heredity of Himself in the flash-point of the soul, and He gives her sex and caprice and free-will to deny herself to Him if she choose; and in her caprice she goes out and away from Him, and when she would return she cannot, because in infidelity she has dropped from perfection. Disillusioned by her unfaithful wanderings and horribly pained, the soul longs for Him, and He longs for her. He Himself must make her the way of return, which is the way of redemption, and at a terrible cost to Himself He shows her His Righteousness and the mode of her Return in the Face and the Ways of Jesus Christ; and in the Crucifixion He shows her the measure of His love, and in the Cross the necessary abandonment of all self-will—total surrender. And all this suffering to Himself He bears in order to make good the willful sinning and the misery of the wayward soul; He brings home the soul, not by force but by love—that love by which He is at once the Life of everything and everything is the life of Him.

God's Gift of Himself
Absence from God is Pain, and everlastingly will be Pain in varying degrees. Are there souls who have never left Him? Undoubtedly, but they know nothing of this world. Are we perhaps distressed at this multiplicity of worlds and souls? We need not be, for they are a necessity both of God and of ourselves; for God to Be Himself He must give Himself, and who can receive Him? Not even the greatest of all the

Angels can alone bear to endure Him? Only into a vast multiplicity of individuals can God pour and expend Himself to the fullness of His desire, the One to the many. Each individually receives from Him, and each individually and collectively—the many to the One—returns Him those burning favors which are in Celestial-living.

Is it all joy to find God? How can it be? Can faults and sins be eradicated without pain? Life here for the lover of God is one long eradication of offences. How can even the daily requirements of flesh be fulfilled without pain? How without profound humiliation and patience can we descend from Contemplation to duties in the household? How without pain consider with that same mind which has so recently been rapt in God—the various merits of breads, pastries, and portions of dead animals, in order that flesh shall eat and live! What a fall is this!—a fall that must be taken daily and patiently. Is it all joy to love God? How can it be? For Love carries in itself a terrible wound of longing which can never be healed till we come before Him in possession Face to Face.

The Soul Homeward Bound

How is it that Perfect Love can consent to the wandering of the soul with its consequent sorrow and sin? Divine Light, being also Perfect Freedom, consents to the wandering of the soul; but Divine Love, being also Reciprocity, may not consent to such wandering as shall forever preclude Reciprocity. The wandering soul must be, will be, Redeemed.

If Divine Light, being also Perfect Freedom, consents to the wandering of the soul, but Divine Love, being also Reciprocity, may not consent to a perpetual wandering, how set limits in a life in which perfect freedom must continue? A limit can be fixed by Evil, Evil the outermost circle from God, the shore on which, continually breaking and being broken, the soul turns herself in longing to a long-forgotten Lord. Evil is the hedge about the vineyard of the Parable. The soul is free to touch it, free to pass through it if she will, but touching it she knows Pain. Pain causes the soul to pause and consider: now is her opportunity; now she is likely to turn about and seek the Good. Then the purpose of Evil is fulfilled; then Evil becomes the handmaid of Good; then we can feel and say with sincerity, Evil has smitten me friendly, for it has caused me to turn about and seek Good. Good, once found, is found to be stronger than Evil. In a few years Good has so drawn us that Evil has become negligible; it lies forgotten on a now distant misty shore. The soul is Homeward bound.

CHAPTER 5
The Romance of the Soul

The Secret Places of God

By what means shall the ordinary man and woman, living the usual everyday life, whether of work or of leisure, find God? And this without withdrawing themselves into a life apart—a "religious" life, and without outward and conspicuous piety always running to public worship (though often very cross and impatient at home); without leaving undone any of the duties necessary to the welfare of those dependent on them; without making themselves in any way peculiar;—how shall these same people go up into the secret places of God, how shall they find the marvelous peace of God, how satisfy those vague persistent longings for a happiness more complete than any they have so far known, yet a happiness which is whispered of between the heart and the soul as something which is to be possessed if we but knew how to get it? How shall ordinary mortals whilst still in the flesh re-enter Eden even for an hour? for Eden is not dead and gone, but we are dead to Eden—Eden, the secret garden of enchantment where the soul and the mind and the heart live in the presence of God and hear once more "the voice of God walking in the garden in the cool of the day" (Genesis 3:8).

It is possible for these things to come to us or we to them, and in quite a few years if we set our hearts on them. First we must desire; and after the desire, steady and persistent, God will give. And we say, "But I have desired and I do desire, and God does not give. Why is this?" There are two reasons for it. For one—are these marvelous things to be given because of one cry; for one petulant demand; for a few tears, mostly of self-pity, shed in an hour when the world fails to satisfy us, when a friend has disappointed us, when our plans are spoiled, when we are sick or lonely? These are the occasions on which we mostly find time to think of what we call a better world, and of the consolations of God.

But let anyone have all that he can fancy, be carried high upon the flood-tide of prosperity, ambition, and success; and how much time will he or she give to Almighty God?—not two moments during the day. Yet the Maker of all things is to bestow His unspeakable riches upon us in return for two moments of our thought or love! Does a man acquire great worldly wealth, or fame, in return for two moments of endeavor?

"Ah," some of us may cry, "but it is more than two moments that I give Him; I give Him hours, and yet I cannot find Him." If that is really so, then the second reason is the one which would explain why He has not been found. A great wall divides us from the consciousness of the Presence of God. In this wall there is one Door, and one only, Jesus Christ. We have not found God because we have not found Him first as Jesus Christ in our own heart. Now whether we take our heart to church, whether we take it to our daily work, or whether we take it to our amusements, we shall not find Jesus in any one place more than another if He is not already in our hearts to begin with. How shall I commence to love a Being whom I have never seen? By thinking about Him; by thinking about Him very persistently; by comparing the world and its friendships and its loves and its deceits and its secret enviousnesses with all that we know of the lovely ways of gentle Jesus. If we do this consistently, it is impossible not to find Him more lovable than any other person that we know. The more lovable we find Him the more we think about Him, by so much the more we find ourselves beginning to love Him, and once we have learnt to hold Him very warmly and tenderly in our heart, then we are well in the way to find the Christ and afterwards that divine garden of the soul in which God seems to slip His hand under our restless anxious heart and lift it high into a place of safety and repose.

When for some time we have learnt to go in and out of this garden, with God's tender help we make ourself a dear place—a nest under God's wing, and yet mysteriously even nearer than this, it is so near to God. To this place we learn to fly to and fro in a second of time: so that, sitting weary and harassed in the counting-house, in an instant a man can be away in his soul's nest; and so very great is the refreshment of it and the strength of it that he comes back to his work a new man, and so silently and quickly done that no one else in the room would ever know he had been there: it is a secret between his Lord and himself.

But the person who learns to do this does not remain the same raw uncivilized creature that once he or she was: but slowly must become quite changed; all tastes must alter (all capacities will increase in an extraordinary manner), and all thoughts of heart and mind must become acceptable and pleasant to God.

It is not the clay of our bodies fashioned by God which makes some common and some not. It is the independent and un-Godlike thoughts of our hearts and minds which can make of us common, and even savage, persons. The changing of these thoughts, the harmonizing of them, and, finally, the total alteration of them, is the work in us of the Holy Spirit. By taking Christ into our hearts and making for Him there a living nest, we set that mighty force in motion which shall eventually make for us a nest in the Living God. For Jesus Christ is able (but only with our own entire *willingness*) to make us not only acceptable to God, but delightful to Him, so much so that even while we remain in the flesh He would seem not to be willing to endure having us always away from Him, but visits us and dwells with us after His own marvelous fashion and catches us up to Himself.

To begin with, we must have a set purpose and *will* towards God. In the whole spiritual advance it is first we who must make the effort, which God will then stabilize, and finally on our continuing to maintain this effort He will bring it to complete fruition. Thus step by step the spirit rises—first the effort, then the gift. First the will to do—and then the grace to do it with. Without the willing will God gives no grace: without God's grace no will of Man can reach attainment. God's will and Man's will, God's love and Man's love—these working and joining harmoniously together raise Man up into Eternal Life.

Inward Meditation

God is desirous of communicating Himself to us in a Personal manner. In the Scriptures we have the foundation, the basis, the cause and reason of our Faith laid out before us; but He wills that we go beyond this basis, this reasoning of Faith, into experience of Himself. For this end, then, He fills us with the aching desire to find and know Him, to be filled with Him, to be comforted and consoled by Him, to discover His joys. He fills us with these desires in order that He may gratify us.

By being willing to receive and understand as only through the medium of the *written* word we limit God in His communications with us. For by the Holy Ghost He will communicate not by written word but by personal touching of love brought about for us by the taking and enclosing of Jesus Christ within the heart not only as the Written Word, the Promise and Hope of Scripture, but as the Living God. For this end inward meditation and pondering are a necessity.

The Exquisite Will of God

What is the true aim of spiritual endeavor—an attempt at personal and individual salvation? Yes, to commence with, but beyond that, and more fully, it is the attempt to comply with the exquisite Will of God; and the general and universal improving and raising of the consciousness of the whole world. Yet this universal improvement must take place in each individual spirit in an individual manner. There are those who would deny to individuality its rights, claiming that the highest spirituality is the total cessation of all individuality; yet this would not appear to be God's view of the matter, for in the most supreme contacts of the soul with Himself He does not wipe out the consciousness of the soul's individual joy, but, on the contrary, to an untellable extent He *increases* it. And Jesus teaches us that life here is both the means and the process of the gradual conformation of the will of Man to the will of God, and our true "work" is the individual learning of this process. But this cultivation of our individuality must not be subverted to the purpose of the mere gain of personal advantage, but because of the heartfelt wish to conform to the glorious will of God. The failure of the human will to run in conjunction with the Divine will is the cause, as we know, of all sin. In the friction of these opposing wills, forces baneful to Man are generated.

On Finding God

From its very earliest commencement in childhood our system of education is based upon wrong ideas. With little or no regard to God's plans Man lays out his own puny laws and ambitions and teaches them to his young. We are not taught that what we are here for is above all and before all to arrive at a sense of personal connection with God, to identify ourselves with the spiritual while still in the flesh. On the contrary, we are taught to grow shy, even ashamed, of the spiritual! and to regard the world as a place principally or even solely in which to enjoy ourselves or make a "successful career."

Happiness! Happiness! We see the great pursuit of it on every side, and no truer or more needful instinct has been given to Man, but he fails to use it in the way intended. This world is a Touchstone, a Finding-place for God. Whoever will obey the law of finding God from this world instead of waiting to try and do it from the next, he, and he only, will ever grasp and take into himself that fugitive mysterious unseen Something which—not knowing what it is, yet feeling that it exists—we have named Happiness.

But how commence this formidable, this seemingly impossible task of finding God in a world in which He is totally invisible? To the "natural" or animal Man God is as totally hidden and inaccessible as He is to the beasts of the field; yet encased within his bosom lies the soul which can be the means of drawing Man and God together in a glorious union. "I have known all this from my childhood," we cry, "and the knowledge of it has not helped me one step upon my way."

Then try again, and reverse your method, for hitherto you have been beseeching gifts from God, asking for gifts from Jesus, and have *forgotten to give*. Give your love to Jesus, give *Him* a home, instead of asking Him to give you one. Give your heart to God, *set it upon Him.*

What is keeping you back? You are afraid of what it will entail; you are afraid of what God will demand of you; those words "Forsake all, and follow Me" fill you with something like terror. I cannot leave my business, my children, my home, my luxuries, my games, my dresses, my friends! Neither need you but, knowing this initial agony of mind, Christ said it is easier for a camel to go through the eye of a needle (the name of an exceedingly narrow gate into Jerusalem) than for a rich man to enter the kingdom of heaven.

What does it mean to "set the heart" upon something? We say, "I have set my heart on going to see my son," "I have set my heart on doing so-and-so," but this does not mean that in order to accomplish it we must wander homeless and lonely until the day of achievement. No; but we set our heart and mind upon eventually accomplishing this wish, we shape all our plans towards it, we give it the first place. This is what God asks us to do; to give Him the first place. We need not go to Him in rags: David and Solomon were immensely wealthy, Job was a rich man; but we must eventually think more of Him than we do of our dress, more of Him than we do of our business, more of Him than we do of lover, friend, or child. Many well-minded people are under the impression that such love for an Invisible Being is a total impossibility. Yet the great commandment stands written all across the face of the heavens—"Thou shalt love Me with all thy heart and mind and soul and strength." Are we then to suppose that God asks the impossible of His own creatures, that He mocks us? No; for when we desire He sends the capacity, and day by day sends us the power to reach this love through Jesus Christ. There is included in the words "Give us this day our daily bread," the bread of the soul, which is Love.

Divine Love commences in us in a very small way, as a very feeble flicker, for we are very feeble and small creatures. But God takes the will for the deed, and the day comes when suddenly we are filled with true love, as a gift. This is indeed the second baptism, the baptism of fire, the baptism of the Holy Ghost; then at last the great wall which has hitherto divided our consciousness from God goes down in its entirety, never again to rise up and divide us. This is the mighty work of Jesus Christ.

Though this is not our work, still we have had the earnest will, the longing desire; we have made continually, perseveringly, our tiny, often futile, efforts to please and place Him first, and though perhaps almost all were failures, He has counted every one to us for righteousness.

To Think on Jesus

We may at all times be asking ourselves, "But how shall I know the will of God, how shall I please Him, how shall I know what Christ would wish me to do or, to think?" There is one test more sure than any other, which is to ask oneself, "Would Jesus have done just this?" and the answer will come from the inward of us instantaneously. But before we can use this test we must have made a careful study of Scripture and also have begun the habit of inward personal intimacy with Jesus Himself. So immense is the bounty of God to the creature that truly and persistently wills and endeavors to please Him, so great are the rewards of that creature for its tiny work that it is as though a child should scratch bare ground with its little spade and reap a harvest of sweet flowers as magic gifts. In this way it is that we find actually fulfilled in ourselves the lovely words of the prophet, "the desert shall blossom like the rose."

The great initial difficulty that surely most of us feel is how to come into personal contact with this Jesus Christ, and to know which are the first steps that we should take to bring about this contact. They are just those same steps that we use to come to a nearer understanding of and greater intimacy with any persons we are desirous of making friends with. We commence by thinking about them, by arranging to spend time in their companionship; and the more we think about them and the more time we spend with them if they are very attractive people, the more we feel in sympathy with them. Form, then, the habit of making for brief instants a mental picture of the Savior. Note the exquisite tenderness of His hands, so instantly ready to save and heal; note the calm strength and the great love in His countenance, walk beside Him down the street, join His daily life, learn to become familiar with Him as Jesus—what would He do, how would He look, what would His thoughts be? To feel sympathetically towards a person is to take one of the most important steps towards friendship. How many of us stop in the rush of our daily amusements, interests, and work to sympathize with Christ? Most probably, if we think of Christ at all, it is to feel that He ought to sympathize with us! Now Christ not only sympathizes with but ardently loves us, and our failure to receive the comfort and help of this love is due to our failure in returning to Him these same feelings of sympathy and love and friendship. We are not reciprocal, but perpetually ask and never give.

"But life is so busy I have no time," you say. What of those hours spent in the train, those moments spent waiting for an appointment, that half-hour taken for a rest, but which is not a rest because of the rushing inharmonious turmoil of your thoughts? No one is so restful to think of as Jesus. Every single quality that we most admire, trust, and love is to be found in Jesus Christ. The only reason of our failure to love Him more ardently than any human being we know is that we do not think enough about Him.

How much offended we should be if anyone dared to say to us, "You are not a Christian." We all consider ourselves Christians as a matter of course; but why this certainty, what reason can we give? Many would say, "I keep the Commandments, and I am baptized in Christ's name." But Christianity is not an act done by hands, it is a life, and the Jews keep the Commandments even more strictly than we and are not Christians. The mere fact of believing that Christ once lived and was crucified is not enough. The Jews and also the Mohammedans believe that He lived and was crucified.

What is then necessary? That we believe that He is indeed the Son of God, the Messiah, the Savior; for if He was no more than a holy man, by what means has He power to save us more than Moses has power to save us?

The true inward knowledge that Christ is God comes not by nature to any man, but by gift of God—which gift must be earnestly sought, striven, prayed for, and desired: this faith is the very coming to God by which we are saved. If we are not yet in this faith that Jesus Christ is the Messiah, then we are neither Jew, Mohammedan, nor Christian, but wanderers without a fold, and without a Shepherd; longing, and not yet comforted.

From the Fleshly to the Spiritual

How do we come by this joy of the personal loving of God, this Romance of the Soul brought to sensible fruition whilst still in the flesh?

Is it a gift? Yes. Is it a gift, because of some merit of goodness on our part beyond the goodness of other persons who are without it, though striving? No. Is it because of some work for God that we do in this world, charitable or social? No. Is it, then, nothing but an arbitrary favoritism on His part? No. Is it a sagacity or cleverness, a height of learning, a result of close study? No.

It is simply and solely a certain and particular obedient attitude of heart and mind towards God of the nature of a longing—giving, a grateful outgoing thinking towards Him, continually maintained, and a heart invitation to, and a receiving of Jesus Christ into ourselves. Our part is to maintain this obedient tender-waiting, giving and receiving attitude under all the circumstances of daily life, and Christ with the Holy Ghost will then work the miracle in us.

What is true religion, what is that religion by which we shall feel *wholly satisfied*? It is to have Christ recognized, known, adored, and living in the soul. This is the New Life within us, this is the New Birth. The first proofs of the power of this New Life in us is the victory over all the lower passions, victory over the animal "that once was ourself"! A victory so complete that not only do we cease to desire those former things or be troubled by them but we no longer "respond" to that which is base, even though we be brought into visual contact with such things as would formerly have inevitably excited at least a passing response in us. Can any man free himself in such a manner from his own nature? Common sense forbids us imagine it. It is then a Living Power within us, slowly transforming us to higher levels, from the fleshly to the spiritual, and shaping us to meet the purity of God. And such is the tender consideration of this Power for our weakness that while we are learning to give up these baser pleasures He teaches us the higher pleasures of the soul—we are not left comfortless. So in our earlier stages we may have many very wonderful ecstasies which later are altogether dispensed with, and indeed are eventually not desired by the soul, or even the more greedy heart and mind, which all now ask and desire one favor only—to be on earth in continual fellowship with Christ Jesus and ever able to enter into the love of God. To be without this glorious power of entering Responsive Love of God, to be cut off from this, is the great and only fear of the soul. This fear it is which holds the soul and the creature towards God both day and night lest by the least forgetfulness or wrongful attitude they should lose Him or displease Him.

All these changes no man can bring about for himself—they are accomplished for him by the Holy Spirit; but this he can and *must* do for himself, invite Sweet Jesus into his heart and enthrone Him there as Ruler. This once accomplished, that mysterious monitor within us commonly known as "Conscience" grows until it attains an excessive sensitiveness which penetrates the minutest acts of life and the deepest recesses of heart and mind. It becomes inexorable, it demands instant and complete obedience. Because of it relations with other persons undergo a drastic change. Complete, instant, entire forgiveness for every offence is demanded, and at last even a momentary annoyance must be effaced; no matter how great the cause of annoyance, it must be effaced in the same instant as that in which it crosses the mind, for a single adverse thought eventually proves as injurious to the Spirit as a grain of sand is to the eyes.

Heaven Is a State of Consciousness

We see on every side men and women who try to fill an emptiness, a wanting that they feel within themselves, by every sort of means except the only one which can ever be a permanent success. Women devote themselves to lovers, husbands, children, dress, society, and dogs; men to business, ambition, the racecourse, folly, drink, games, and arts. Are any of these persons truly happy, truly satisfied in all their being? No, and they descend to old age surrounded by the dust of disillusionment. Lonely and soon forgotten by the hungry pleasure-seeking crowd, such persons pass from this world, and the most their friends have to say is that they have gone to a better one. But have they? For the mere fact of shedding the flesh does not bring us any nearer to God. On the contrary, this world is the very place in which we can most easily and quickly get into communication with God.

To think that the mere act of dying improves our character and takes us to heaven is a delusion of the Enemy—it is living here which can fit us and carry us to heaven; and we have no great distance to travel either, for heaven is a state of consciousness, and by entering that state of consciousness we become united and connected with such degrees of heaven as the flesh is able to bear, though these degrees fall infinitely short of those required by the soul: hence the fearful hungering and longing of the soul to depart from the flesh. If we do not find Christ whilst we are here, when we cast off the flesh we enter a bewildering vortex of a life of terrible intensity and great solitude. We are aware of nothing but Self, are tormented by Self with its forever unsatisfied longings, and by the *impossibility of achieving any other Self*. In this intensity of self-tormenting loneliness the soul feels to gyrate, and all that she knows of that which is outside of this Self is the sound of the rushing of invisible things, for she is blind without the light of this world and without the light of Christ. The joys of space are not open to her, only the dark and lonely horrors of it: she is in an incalculably greater state of isolation from God than here in this world! The remedy for all this lies here; let no one think he can afford to wait to find this remedy until after he leaves this world, for then his chance is gone, and who is able to foretell when it will return? What can be more beautiful, more happy, than to find this remedy, to find the only Being who loves us as much as we love ourselves: the gentle, tender, gracious, all-sufficing Christ; that all-mighty ever-giving Christ who yearns over and longs for us—what madness is it that prevents us seeking Him?

If the natural man were asked, "What is life? what is it to live?" he would reply, "It is to eat, drink, laugh, love, and have pleasure or pain: to hear, see, touch, taste and smell, and to be conscious that I do all these things." Yet this consciousness is but a tiny speck of consciousness, and some mysterious voice within the deeply-thinking man tells him that this is so. But how uncover a further consciousness? This is the secret of the soul.

To pass from one form of consciousness to another—this is to increase life fifty, a hundred, a thousand times according to the degrees of consciousness we can attain. These degrees would seem to be irrevocably limited because of the mechanical actions of heart and breathing, which automatic actions become suspended or seriously interfered with in very high states of consciousness. When first these very great expansions of consciousness take place, the creature is under strong conviction that the soul has left the body—that it has gone upon some mysterious journey—this because of several reasons. The first is because of a certain persistent sound of rushing; the second is because of the sense of living at tremendous speed, in a manner previously altogether unknown and totally undreamed of, in which the senses of the body have no concern whatever and are completely closed down; thirdly, on returning from this "journey" we are not immediately able to exact obedience from the body, which remains inert and stiffly cold and suffers distress with too slow breathing. But reason demands, "How is it possible that the soul should leave the body and the body not die? and also we perceive this, that, though the consciousness is projected to an infinite distance, or includes that infinite distance within itself, it yet remains aware of the existence of the body, though very dimly."

The method employed, then, for administering these experiences to the soul and the creature is not by means of drawing the soul out of the body, but by a withdrawal of the condition of insulation from Divine Life, in which insulation all creatures have their normal existence, which may be termed a state of total Unawareness. By Will of God this condition of insulation is removed, the soul enters Connection and becomes instantly and vividly aware of Spiritual Life and of that which Is, at an infinite distance from herself, so that the soul is at one and the same time in paradise or heaven, and upon the earth: space is eaten up. Without seeing or hearing, the soul partakes in a tremendous and unspeakable manner of the joys of God, which, all unfelt by us as "natural" man, pass unceasingly throughout the universe.

These experiences give an immense and unshakable knowledge to the soul and the creature of the immense reality of the Unseen Life, and are doubtless sent us to effect this knowledge. Why, then, is not every man given this knowledge? Because the creature must qualify before being allowed to receive it, and too many hold back from the tests. By these experiences we learn some little portion of the mystery which lies between the pettiness of that which we now are and the great glories that we shall come to; and in this awful heavenly mystery in which are fires that have no flame, and melody which has no sound, the soul is drawn to Everlasting Love. But we cannot endure the bliss of it, and the soul prays to be covered on account of the creature.

The God-Conscious Life

Incessant work is the lot of the awakened and returning soul, and justly so, for because of what folly and ingratitude did she ever leave God? A multiplicity of choices lie before her, and her great concern is which amongst all these possible decisions will prove the shortest path to God. These choices and decisions must be brought down to the meanest details of everyday life. At first on awakening the soul would like nothing better than to forsake and cast away material things altogether, and is inclined to despise the body. But Jesus teaches her that this is not pleasing: it is His Will that she should continually lend assistance to the creature in its weaknesses and uncertainties, not disdaining it but helping it. It is the soul which maintains contact with the Divine Guide, and then in turn should guide the creature. As the Divine Guide condescends to the soul, never despising her, so must the soul condescend to the creature: acknowledging and understanding that nothing is too small or humble for the soul to attend to and lead the creature to do in a beautiful and gentle manner. By these means the permeation of the natural world by the Divine is carried out, and no act or fact of life can be considered too insignificant for the soul to attend to for the development of this aim.

The life of conscious connection with God is true living as far as we may know it in the flesh, an enormous increase over the petty normal life of the world or, more rightly, the petty and *lacking* life of the world. For in this life of God-consciousness is an immense sanity and poise, a balance between soul and body and heart and mind never achieved in the "normal" or "natural" life. Therefore the God-conscious life is not to be named an abnormal but the complete, full, and only truly normal life: a life in which both soul and creature have found their center, and the whole being in all its parts is brought to evenness, to harmony, to peace, and a greatly magnified intelligence. If all men and women attained this state, this world would automatically become Paradise. In this true life living and feeling alter their characteristics and surpass anything that can be imagined by the uninitiated mind.

Now, though to convey some idea of this condition of consciousness would seem to be impossible, still there are some types of persons to whom a little something of the commencement of the larger life of the awakened soul might be conveyed before they themselves experience it. The lovers of nature, of music, of the beautiful and romantic, and of poetry: in the highest moments reached by such they are aware of an indefinable Something—an expansion, a going out towards, a longing—yearning, subtly composed of both joy and pain, which goes beyond the earth, beyond the music, beyond the poetry, beyond the beautiful into a Nameless Bourne. At these moments they live with the soul: this is the commencement of spirit-life. When the Nameless Bourne has become to the soul that which It really is—God—and *He sends His responses to her*, then the soul knows the fullness of spiritual life as we may know it in the flesh.

But she can neither know the Nameless Bourne as God nor receive His responses till the heart and the mind have come to repentance of their ways and have been changed at least in part. Without this mode of living no one can be said to live in a full or whole manner, because nothing is whole which does not include the consciousness of God, and this in a lively and acute degree.

The Fullness of the Finding of God
One of our great difficulties is that when, as the merely half-repentant creature, we turn to God and, beginning to ask favors of Him, get no response, then all our warm feelings and longings towards Him fall back, we go into a state either of profounder unbelief (which is further separation) or into total apathy. Apathy is a deadly thing. The more God loves us the more He will do His part to keep us from it. All the circumstances of life will be used to this end. We may lose our nearest and dearest. If it is material prosperity that causes a too complete content to live without Him, then some or all of that prosperity will be removed. In whatever spot we are most tender—there He will touch us. "Oh, if it had been anyone else or anything less that we had lost, then it would not have been so hard to bear," we say. Exactly. For nothing less would have been of any use, and alas! even this may be of no use, for Christ is ever willing and trying to save us, and we will not be saved.

We cannot in one step mount up out of our faithless indifferent wrongful condition into the glories of the knowledge of God. First we must learn to know Jesus, intimately, devotedly. Then Jesus the Christ: then the Father. Finally God the Holy Trinity, once found and known by us, becomes our All, and by some unspeakable condescension He becomes to us all things in all ways. The soul is filled with romantic and divine love, and instantly God is her Holy Lover: she is sad, weary, or afraid, and immediately she turns to Him and He comforts and mothers her: she is filled with adoring filial love, and at once He is her Father. Oh, the wonders of the fullness of the finding and knowing of God!

An Invisible Will

Let the man who would know happiness here study the works of God, and not think he will gain virtue by putting everything that he sees here upon one side, saying it is not real or it is not good. It is very real of its own kind, and good also if he learns how to use it, and very marvelous. Let him study how things are made—God's things, not trivial man-made things—let him observe how all are made with equal care, the humblest and the proudest, "the tiny violet perfect as the oak." Let him learn the manner of the ways of light and the colors of all that he sees, and then stop to consider how, having made all these marvels, God then fashioned his own delicate eyes that he might see and know and enjoy them all. To consider all these things, accepting them from God with love, makes the heart and the mind and the soul dance and sing together not with noise but like sunshine upon water.

What is Nature but the demonstration in visible objects of an invisible Will? This Will we need to trace to its Source; having done this, we are able to praise and bless God for every single thing of beauty He has fashioned here: and this praising and blessing of God becomes nothing less than a continual ecstasy for both soul and creature, and, indeed, because of this and by means of this burning appreciation of God's works, both soul and creature find their sweetest consolations as they wait to be taken to a holier world. When they both bless God with the fire of their love for every tender thing that He has made, then their days become to them one long delight.

We Are a Great Want

We are made to love and adore God, and because of this without Him we are an Emptiness, a Great Want. Such is the lovely and perfect reciprocity of love that as this Great Want we are the pleasure and the joy of the All-Giving God. And He is the All-Giving that He may rejoice and fill our extremity of Want. So we are each to each that which each most desires. This is Divine Love.

Do not let us imagine that by making very much of earthly loves we shall by that obtain the heavenly: on the contrary, love of creatures, and too much turning to and thinking of and depending upon creatures, is a sure manner of hindering us *till* we have learnt to unite with Divine Love. This is not to say that we are not to love our fellow-creatures, attend to them, wait upon them, bear with them, and work for them; but whilst doing all these we are not to make them the object of our life: we are not to think that by merely running about amongst creatures frenzied with plans for their social improvement and comfort the nearer we are necessarily getting to God, or even truly pleasing Him. All these multiplicities of frenzied interests are best centered upon the finding and knowing and loving of Jesus Christ within our own hearts. When this finding, knowing, loving, and believing has been accomplished, then we shall have accomplished the only work God asks us to accomplish, and all other works will automatically, peacefully, and smoothly come to their proper fruition in us through Him.

Neither imagine we shall do this finding of Jesus in, or because of, another person. We shall not find Him in another person or anywhere till we have first found Him in ourselves: and this by inward pondering, delicate tender thinkings, loving comparisons, sweet enthusiasms, and persistent endeavors to imitate His gentle ways and manners. The need which is the most pressing of all our needs is to find that Light which will light us when we have to go out from the light of this world into the awful solitudes of that which we often so lightly and confidently speak of as "the other world." Without Christ we go out into a fearful loneliness: with Christ we walk the rainbow paths of Paradise.

Of Church Ceremonials

What are the blisses of God? They are contact with an immeasurable Ardor, they are our ardor meeting the Fountain of all Ardors: and God is communicated to us by a magnetism which in its higher degrees becomes luminous and unbearable. Are these divine joys and comforts of God towards us because we are more loved by God, because our salvation is more sure than that of those who are without these comforts? Most emphatically no. It is because we obey a particular and subtle law of giving to God, and do not (as is more natural to us) content ourselves with merely believing, expecting, and hoping to receive *from* God.

On every side we hear complaints against the Church. It is suggested that we are falling away from God because of some lack in the Church. But this fault of the Church is exactly the same fault which is to be found in the members of the congregation which compose it—a tepid love for a dimly known Lord. When the priest and every member of the congregation in his own heart worships the beloved Christ, then the Church will be found to have gained just that which is now lacking, and which we attribute to some priestly failure and not our own also.

Of Church ceremonials it is hard to speak, for the lover of God can have no eyes for them: he is all heart, but sees it this way—that set rules, regulations, and ceremonials in prayers and worship are most right and proper for the creature publicly worshipping its Creator. That the assembling together in church is the outward and visible acknowledgment of the creature's worship of God and also a looking for the fulfilling of the promise "where two or three are gathered together in My name." The redeemed creature worships very ardently with all its little heart and mind and all its tiny strength, learning in its own self the words of David: "I was glad when they said unto me, We will go into the house of the Lord." But the soul cannot worship in set words, neither can she have need or use for the ceremonials invented by and for the creature, but worships God in another manner altogether, as she is taught by the Holy Spirit, and in the greatness of her worship mounts to God, and closes with God. For holy love cannot long be divided.

When holy love grows great in us we wonder that we ever thought that human love was love at all, for no matter how great it may once have seemed it now seems so small it is no greater than the humming of a bee around a flower in summer time. But holy love—who can commence to describe it? It rides upon great wings, it burns like a devouring fire, it makes nothing of Space and comes before Him like the lightnings, saying, "Here am I," and, gathering all things, all loves into itself, pours them out at the feet of God.

The Intelligence of the Soul

Above the fretful and contentious human reason is the intelligence of the soul, and this soul has in itself a higher part, for we become acutely aware of it—that part of it with which we come in contact with God, with which we respond to God, receive His manifestations, are laid bare to His blisses. Separated from worldly things by an impalpable veil, it rests above all such things in serene calm, and, strangest of all, has no comprehension whatever of sin: when we enter this part of the soul and live with it sin and evil become not only non-existent, but unthinkable, unimaginable: we are totally removed from any such order of existence. It communicates its knowledge to the lower part of the soul, the soul to the Reason, the Reason to the rest of the creature.

We say we are fearfully and wonderfully made, and in saying this we think of the body, but far more wonderful is the making of the spiritual of us. O man, climb out of the gross materialism of thy fleshly self, for thou canst do it! As out of the heavy earth come the delicate flowers of spring, so out of the heavy body, because of *that divine* which is within it, come the marvelous flowers of the soul.

Of the Blessed Sacrament

Nothing is of a deeper mystery or difficulty or disappointment to the soul and the heart well advanced in the experience and in the love of God than to find that in the ceremony of the Blessed Sacrament it is possible for them to be less sensible of receiving from God than at any time. How and why can this be? Is it the Ceremonial causing the mind to be too much alert to guide the body now to rise, now to kneel, now to move in some direction? Is it this distraction which prevents perception—for in all communion with God the mind is closed down, the heart and soul only being in operation? On the other hand, it is easily possible to be in closest communion with God in all the noises and distractions of a great railway station, amongst a crowd of shifting persons. No, it is some imperfection in the attitude, adopted by the heart and mind in approaching this Sacrament. In what way have we perhaps been approaching it? In an attitude of awe accompanied by a humble expectancy or hope of receiving. We hope and believe we shall receive God's grace. Now, what were our Lord's words? He said, "Do this in remembrance of Me," or more correctly translated, "Do or offer this as a memorial of Me before God." This implies an act of giving upon our part, whereas we have come to regard this ceremony as an act of receiving.

Although the attitude of humble expectancy to receive is of itself a worthy one it does not fulfill the exact command, which is to commemorate, offer, and hold up before God the Perfect Love and Sacrifice of our Savior, as a living memorial of Him before God. It should be accompanied by an offering of great love and thanks upon our part without regard to anything we may receive. But because first we give we then receive.

We have nothing to give to God but our love, thanks, and obedience; but of these it is possible to give endlessly, and the more we give the more God-like do we become, and the more God-like the higher and further do we enter into the great riches and blisses of God. On going to partake of the Blessed Sacrament we do well to banish from the heart and mind all thought of what it may please God to still further give *us* and to make an offering *to* God. The only way we can make an offering to God is upon the wings of love, and upon this love we hold up before Him the bread and wine as the Body and Blood of our Redeemer, repeating and repeating in our heart, "I eat and drink This as a memorial before Thee of the Perfect Love and Sacrifice of Jesus Christ." When we so do with *great* love in our heart we find that we are able sensibly to receive great grace.

Modes of Prayer

Of the many kinds and degrees of prayer first perhaps we learn the prayer of the lips, then that of the mind, then the prayer of the heart, and finally the prayer of the soul—prayer of a totally different mode and order, prayer of a strange incalculably great magnetic power, prayer which enables us to count on help from God as upon an absolute and immediate certainty.

We find this about perfect prayer that it is not done as from a creature beseeching a Creator at an immense distance, but is done as a love-flash which, eating up all distance, is immediately before and with the Creator and is accompanied by vivid certainty at the heart; this latter is active faith; we have too much perhaps of that kind of faith which may be named waiting or passive faith.

This combination of love with active faith instantly opens to us God's help. We may or may not receive this in the form anticipated by the creature, but later perceive that we have received it in exactly that form which would most lastingly benefit us. After a while we cease almost altogether from petitioning anything for ourselves, having this one desire only: that by opening ourselves to God by means of offering Him great love, we receive Himself.

An Infusion of God-Energy

To enter the contemplation of God is not absence of will, nor laziness of will, but great energy of will because of, and for, love: in which love-condition the energy of the soul will be laid bare to the energy of God, the two energies for the time being becoming closely united or oned, in which state the soul-will or energy is wholly lifted into the glorious God-Energy, and a state of unspeakable bliss and an *immensity* of *living* is immediately entered and shared by the soul. Bliss, ecstasy, rapture, all are energy, and according as the soul is exposed to lesser or greater degrees of this energy, so she enters lesser or greater degrees of raptures.

It is misleading in these states of ecstasy to say that the soul has vision, if by vision is to be understood anything that has to do with concrete forms or any kind of sight; for the soul is totally blind. But she makes no account of this blindness and has her fill of all bliss and of the knowledge of another manner of living without any need whatever of sight. Has the wind eyes or feet? yet it possesses the earth and is not prevented. So the soul, without eyes and without hands, possesses God.

Contact with God is then of the nature of the Infusion of Energy. The infusions of this energy may take the form of causing us to have an acute intense perception and consciousness (but not such form of perception as would permit us to say "I saw," but a magnetic inward cognizance, a fire of knowledge which scintillates about the soul and pierces her) of His perfections; of His tenderness, His sweetness, His holiness, His beauty. When either of these last two are made known to her, the soul passes into what can only be named as an agony of bliss, insupportable even to the soul for more than a very brief time, and because of the fearful stress of it the soul draws away and prays to be covered from the unbearable happiness of it, this being granted her whether automatically (that is to say, because of spiritual law) or whether by direct and merciful will of God—who is able to tell?

Contemplation, even in its highest forms, is not to be confused with spiritual "experiences," which are totally apart from anything else that we may know in life—they are entirely outside of our volition, they are not to be prayed for, they are not to be even secretly desired, but to be accepted how and when and if God so chooses.

In contemplation the will is used, and we are not able to come to it without the will is penetratingly used towards the joining and meeting with the will and love of God. In the purely spiritual "experience" from first to last there is no will but an absence of will, a total submission and yielding to God, without questioning, without fear, without curiosity, and the only will used is to keep ourselves in willingness to submit to whatever He shall choose to expose us to. God does not open to us such experiences in order to gratify curiosity—but expecting that we shall learn and profit by them. First we find them an immense and unforgettable assurance of another form of living, of great intensity, at white heat, natural to a part of us with which we have hitherto been unfamiliar (the soul) but inimical to the body, which suffers grievously whilst the soul glows with marvelous vitality and joy.

This assurance of another manner of living, though we see nothing with the eyes, is the opening of another world to us. But we are not given and shown these mysteries without paying a price: we must learn to live in extraordinary lowliness and loneliness of spirit. The interests, enjoyments, pastimes of ordinary life dry up and wither away. It becomes in vain that we seek to satisfy ourselves in any occupation, in anything, in any persons, for God wills to have the whole of us. When He wills to be sensibly with us, all Space itself feels scarcely able to contain our riches and our happiness. When He wills to disconnect us from this nearness, there is nothing in all the universe so poor, so destitute, so sad, so lonely as ourself. And there is no earthly thing can beguile or console us, because, having tasted of God, it is impossible to be satisfied or consoled save inwardly by God Himself. But He opens up Nature to us in a marvelous way, unbelievable until experienced. He offers us Nature as a sop to stay our tears. By means of Nature He even in absence caresses the soul and the creature, speaks to them fondly, encourages and draws them after Him, sending acute and wonderful perceptions to them, so that, quite consoled, they cry aloud to Him with happiness. And often when the creature is alone and secure from being observed by anyone He will open His glamour to the soul and she passes into union with paradise and even more—high heaven itself. These are angels' delights which He lavishes upon the prodigal.

The Glamour of God and Glamour of Evil

The heart and soul are subject to four principal glamours: the glamour of youth, the glamour of romance, the glamour of evil, and the glamour of God. When once the Spirit of Love, which is God, descends into our soul then a new light becomes created in us by which we see the glamour of evil in its true form and complexion. We see it as disease, misery, imprisonment, and death; and who finds it difficult to turn away from such? The natural man sees evil as an intense attraction, the spiritual man as a horror of ugliness. See then how the Spirit of Love is at once and easily our Salvation.

Amongst all mysteries none seems greater to us than the mystery of Evil. God—Goodness—Love: these we understand. But evil—whence and why, since God is Love, Omnipotence, and Holiness? We cannot but observe that all things have their opposites: summer and winter, heat and cold, light and dark, silence and sound, pleasure and pain, life and death, action and repose, joy and sadness, illness and health; and how shall we know or have true pleasure in the one without we have also knowledge of the opposite? The man who has never known sickness has neither true gratitude, understanding, nor pleasure in his heart over his good health: he does not know that which he possesses. Neither can we know the great glory that is Holiness till we have known evil and can contrast the two.

"But what a price to pay for knowledge; what fearful risk and danger to His creatures for God so to teach them!" we may cry, forgetting that with God all things are possible, "Who is able and strong to save." And does He dare set Himself no difficult thing that He may overcome it? The strong man's knowledge of his own courage forbids us think it. God wills to save us. We have but to join our will with His, and we are saved. How shall we mount to God other than by mounting upon that which offers a foundation of tangible resistance, overcoming and mounting upon evil. Evil then becomes our stairway—the servant of Good. By using the evil that we meet with day by day, we mount daily the nearer to God by that exact degree of evil which we have overcome by good—that is to say, by practice of forgiveness, compassion, patience, humility, endurance, held out over against the invitation of evil to do the exact opposite. Truly if we have

93

the will to use it, Evil is friendly. If we misuse Evil—that is to say, if we do not use it by mounting on it but, intoxicated with its glamour, consent to it, this is Sin, and immediately the stairway is not that of ascent but of descent and death.

The Master says "Resist not evil." How are we to understand this but by assuming that if we try our strength against Evil, Evil is likely to overcome us? but on being confronted with Evil we should instantly hold on to and join with the forces of Good and so have strength quietly to continue side by side with Evil without being seduced by it. When Evil cannot seduce—that is to say, make us consent to it—then for us it is conquered. When we give in or conform to this seduction we generate Sin. Let us say that we are in temptation, that Evil of some sort confronts and invites us; if we battle with this presentment, this picture, this insinuating invitation held out before us by Evil, the act of contending with the invitation will fix it all the more firmly in our minds. We need to substitute another picture, another invitation, another presentment, of that which pertains to the good and the beautiful. He who has learnt so to substitute and present before his own heart and mind Jesus and the pure and beautiful invitations of this Divine Jesus can solve the difficulty. This is not contending, this is substituting; this is transferring allegiance from the glamour of Evil which is present with us, to the glamour of God, which, because we are in temptation, is not present, but is yet hoped and waited for.

Of all false things nothing is more false than the glamour of Evil, for when on being drawn into it we sin, instead of the hoped-for delight we soon find satiety; instead of exhilaration, fatigue; instead of contentment, disillusion; instead of satisfaction, dust; instead of romance, the greedy claws of the harpy; and the further we go in response to this glamour the more pitiable our outlook; for the sweets and possibilities of Evil are extraordinarily limited. Can any man devise a new sin? No, but ever pursues the same old round, the same pitiful circle.

If we pursue the glamour of God, we find the exact opposite of all these things. Spiritual delights know no satiety because of infinite variety: they know no disease, no disillusionment, and who can set a boundary or limit to the beautiful, to love, and light, and God?

The Poignancy of Temptations

It is characteristic of temptation that while we are exposed to it Christ is absent from perception; for to perceive Christ would instantly free us from all temptation (and often it is by temptation faithfully borne that we mount). When we are in a condition of contact with Christ which is His grace, we are raised above the stem of faith into the flowers of knowledge; but for the true strengthening of the will it is necessary that we live also on the harder and more difficult meat of faith. So we return again and again to that insulation from things heavenly in which we lived before we had been made Aware. When we emerge from these dark periods we find ourselves to have advanced. With regard to Grace we can neither truly receive nor benefit by it without our heart, mind, and soul are previously adjusted to Response to it.

The regenerated creature is not exempt from further temptations, but contrariwise the poignancy of these temptations is greatly increased (though of a quite different order of temptation to that known to us in an unregenerated state); it is increased in proportion to the degrees of Grace vouchsafed to us. That is to say, temptation keeps level with our utmost capacity of resistance yet never is allowed to exceed the bounds, for when it would exceed them a way out is found by the return of Grace; and we are freed. The cause is the great root called Self, a hydra-headed growth of selfishness, both material and spiritual, sprouting in all directions. We would seem to be here forever enclosed as in a glass bottle with this most horrid growth. Through the glass we see all life, but always and ever in company with this voracious Self. No sooner do we lop off one shoot of it than another grows—never was such strenuous gardening as is required to keep this growth in check, and every time we lop a shoot we learn another pain. This is the long road to perfection, for the Cross is "I" with a stroke through it.

The Magnetic Power of Grace

As a man's desire is so is he. If our desire is entirely towards fleshly things and joys and comforts, we are sensualists. If our desire is all towards sport and horses, we are not above horses but rather below them, for the human animal is full of guile and the horse of obedience and generosity. Nevertheless he is no goal for the human to aim at. If we desire the beautiful, we become beautified and refined. If we desire God, we become godly.

It is characteristic of spiritual progress that each step is gained through suffering, through penetrating faithful endeavors, through grievous incomprehensible turmoils and discords of the spirit, worked frequently by means of the everyday commonplace happenings and responsibilities of our daily life; and finally as each new step is gained we are by Grace carried to it in a flood of divine happiness to crown our woes. Grace is God's magnetic power acting directly and immediately upon us and is altogether independent of place, time, services, sacraments, or ceremonies. We limit God's communication with us in this way—that He is communicable to us only in so far as we ourselves respond and are able, apt, and willing to receive Him.

Is the condition of blessed nearness to God permanent? No, not as a condition but as a capacity only. We have need to perpetually renew this condition by a positive active enthusiasm toward God. We can in laziness no more retain and use this condition as a permanency than we can sleep one night and eat one meal and have these suffice for our lifetime. But slowly, with work and with pain, we learn perpetually to regain this condition by that form of prayer which is the spiritual breathing-in of the Spirit of Christ.

To look up by day or night into the vastness of the sky with its endless depths, and as we do it burn with the consciousness of God, this is to truly live. No distance is too great, no space too wide. All is our home. Without this burning consciousness of God, Space is a thing of fear and Eternity not to be thought of.

A Spiritual Back-Water
Of the many experiences and conditions of the soul returning to God there is a condition all too easily entered—that of an enervating, pulseless, seductive inertia. In this condition of inert but marvelous contentment the soul would love to stay. This is spiritual sensuality, a spiritual back-water. The true life and energy of the soul are lulled to idleness: basking in happiness, the soul ceases to give and becomes merely receptive.

This condition is entered from many levels: we can rise to it (for it is very high) from ordinary levels, branch side-ways to it from high contemplation; drop to it from the greatest contacts with God. This condition seems strangely familiar to the soul. So much so that she questions herself. Was it from this I started on my wanderings from God? The true health of the soul when in the blisses of God is to be in a state of intense living or activity. She is then in perfect connection with the Divine Energy. She is then in a state of an immense and boundless radiantly joyful Life.

Goodness Is Greater Than Evil

To find God is to have the scope of all our senses increased, but it is easily to be understood that our power of suffering increases also, because we are, as it were, flayed and laid bare to everything alike. But it increases our joys to so great a degree that for the first time in life joy is greater than pain, happiness is greater than sorrow, knowledge is greater than fear, and Good suddenly becomes to us so much greater than Evil that Evil becomes negligible. This increase, this wonderful addition to our former condition, might be partly conveyed by comparison to a man who from birth has never been able to appreciate music: for him it has been meaningless, a noise without suggestion, without delight, without wings, and suddenly by no powers of his own the immense charms and pleasures and capacities of it are laid open to him! These increases of every sense and faculty God will give to His lovers, so that without effort and by what has now become to us our own nature we are continually able to *enter the Sublime*.

Of the Two Wills

We have in us two wills. The Will to live, and the Will to love God and to find Him. The first will we see being used continually and without ceasing, not only by every man, woman, and child, but by every beast of the field and the whole of creation. The Will to live is the will by which all alike seek the best for themselves, here gaining for themselves all that they can of comfort and well-being out of the circumstances and opportunities of life. This is our natural Will. But it is not the will which gains for us Eternal Life, nor does it even gain for us peace and happiness during this life. It is this Will to live which in Christ's Process we are taught to break and bruise till it finally dies, and the Will to love, and gladly and joyously to please God is the only Will by which we live.

Our great difficulty is that we try at one and the same time to hang to God with the soul and to the world with our heart. What is required is not that we go and live in rags in a desert place, but that in the exact circumstances of life in which we find ourselves we learn in *everything to place God first*. He requires of us a certain subtle and inward fidelity—a fidelity of the heart, the will, the mind. The natural state of heart and mind in which we all normally find ourselves is to have temporary vague longings for something which, though indefinable we yet know to be better and more satisfying than anything we can find in the world. This is the soul, trying to overrule the frivolity of the heart and mind and to re-find God. Our difficulties are not made of great things, but of the infinitely small—our own caprices. Though we can often do great things, acts of surprising heroism, we are held in chains—at once elastic and iron—of small capricious vanities, so that in one and the same hour we may have wonderful, far-reaching aspirations towards the Sublime, and God; and yet there comes a pretty frock, a pleasant companion, and behold God is forgotten! The mighty and marvelous Maker of the Universe, Lord of everything, is placed upon one side for a piece of chiffon, a flattering word from a passing lover.

So be it. He uses no force. We are still in the Garden of Free-Will. And when the Garden closes down for us, what then? Will chiffon help us? Will the smiles of a long-since faithless lover be our strength? Now is the time to decide; but our decision is made in the world, and by means of the world and not apart from it, and in the exact circumstances in which we find ourselves.

An Ineffable Tenderness

Another difficulty we have, and which forms an insuperable barrier to finding God, is the ever-recurring—we may almost say the continual—secret undercurrent of criticism and hardness towards God over what we imagine to be His Will. We need to seek God with that which is most like Him, with a will which most nearly resembles His own. To be in a state of hardness or criticism, not only for God but for any creature, in even the smallest degree is to be giving allegiance to, and unifying ourselves with, that Will which is opposite to, furthest away from, and opposed to God. He Himself is Ineffable Tenderness.

Having once re-found God, the soul frequently cries to Him in an anguish of pained wonder, "How could I ever have left Thee? How could I ever have been faithless to Thine Unutterable Perfections?" This to the soul remains the mystery of mysteries. Was it because of some imperfection left in her of design by God in order that He might enjoy His power to bring her back to Him? If this were so, then every single soul must be redeemed—and not for love's sake, but for His Honor, His own Holy Name, His Perfection. If the soul left

Him because of a deliberate choice, a preference for imperfection, a poisonous curiosity of foreign loves, then love alone is the cause and necessity of our redemption, and so it feels to be, for in experience we find that love is the beginning and the middle and the end of all His dealings with us.

Service and Self-Surrender

What is our part and what is our righteousness in all this Process of the Savior? This—that we obey, and that we renounce our own will, accepting and abiding by the Will of God: and this self-lending, self-surrender, this sacrifice of self-will is counted to us for sufficient righteousness to merit heavenly life. But from first to last we remain conscious that we have no righteousness of our own, that we are very small and full of weaknesses, and remain unable to think or say, "This is my righteousness, I am righteous," any more than a man standing bathed in, or receiving the sunlight can say or think, "I am the sun." Is all this, then, as much as to say that we can sit down and do nothing; but, leaving all to Christ, we merely believe, and because of this believing our redemption is accomplished? No, for we have an active part to play, a part that God never dispenses with—the keeping of the will in an active state of practical obedience, submission, and humble uncomplaining endurance through every kind of test. But through it all it is the Great Physician Himself who cures, and we are no more able to perform these changes of regeneration in heart than a critical operation on our own body. So He takes our vanities and, one by one, strews them among the winds, and we raise no protest; takes our prides and breaks them in pieces, and we submit; takes our self-grati-fications and reduces them to dust, and we stand stripped but patient; takes the natural lusts of the creature and transfigures them to Holy Love. And in all this pain of transition, what is the Divine Anesthetic that He gives us? His Grace.

Having submitted to all that Christ esteems necessary for our regeneration, what does He set us to? Service. Glad, happy service to all who may need it. He has wonderful ways of making us acquainted with His especial friends, and it pleases Him to make us the means of answering the prayers of His poor for help, to their great wonder and joy and to the increase of their faith in Him. Also He uses us as a human spark, to ignite the fires of another man's heart: when He uses us in this way, it will seem to one like the opening of a window—to another a magnetism. One will see it as a light flashed on dark places, another receives it as the finding of a track where before was no track. But however many times we may be used in this way, the working remains a mystery to us.

What is our reward whilst still in this world for our patient obediences and renunciations? This—that all becomes well with us the moment the process is brought to the stage where the aim of our life ceases to be the enjoyment of worldly life and becomes fixed upon the Invisible and upon God: and all this by and because of love, for it is love alone which can make us genuinely glad to give up our own will and which can keep us from sinning.

We commence by qualifying through our human love, meager and fluctuating as it is, for God's gift of holy love—of divine reciprocity, and with the presentation of this divine gift immediately we find ourselves in possession of *a new set of desires*, which for the first time in our experience of living prove themselves completely satisfying in fruition. God does not leave us in an arid waste, because He would have us to be holy, and nowhere are there such ardent desires as in heaven; but He transposes and transfigures the carnal desires into the spiritual by means of this gift of divine reciprocity which is at once access to and union with Himself. Now, and only now do we find the sting pulled out of every adverse happening and every woe of life, and out of death also.

The Lover of God
Though from earliest childhood we may have found in the beauties of Nature a great delight, when we become the lover of God He passes His fingers over our hearts and our eyes and opens them to marvelous new powers for joy. Oh, the ecstasy that may be known in one short walk alone with God! The over-flowing heart cries out to Him, What other lover is there can give such bliss as this, and what is all Nature but a lovely language between Thee and me! Then the soul spreads wings into the blue and sings to Him like soaring lark.

But do not let us seek Him only because of His Delights, for so we might miss Him altogether. But let it be because it is His wish: because Perfection calls, and mystery calls to mystery, and love to love, and Light calls to the darkness and the Dawn is born.

The Romance of the Soul

The glamour of God is come down about my soul,
And He who made all loveliness has decked my heart in spring,
And garlanded me round about with tender buds,
Of flowers and scented things, and love and light.
I see no rain, no sad gray skies,
For the glamour of God has come down about mine eyes,
And the Voice of the Maker of all loveliness
Calling to my soul, leads me enchanted
Up the glittering mysteries of Infinity.

CHAPTER 6
The Golden Fountain

The Pearl of Great Price
How many of us inwardly feel a secret longing to find God; and this usually accompanied by the perception that we are confronted by an impenetrable barrier—we cannot find Him—we can neither go through this barrier nor climb over it! We have faith. We are able to admit that He exists, for we cannot help but perceive a Will dominating the laws of the Universe; but something deep within us that we cannot put a name to, something subtle, secret, and strange, cries aloud, "But I need more than this, it is not enough; I need personally to find and know Him. Why does he not permit me to do so?"

We might easily answer ourselves by remembering that if, in everyday life, we greatly desire to see a friend, our best way of doing so is by going in the direction in which he is to be found: we should consider this as obvious. Then let us apply this, which we say is so obvious, to God. We waste too much time looking for Him in impossible directions and by impossible means. He is not to be found by merely studying lengthy arguments, brilliant explanations of theological statements, or controversies upon the meanings of obscure dogmas. He is not even to be found through organizing charity concerts and social reforms however useful. We shall find Him through a self stripped bare of all other interests and pretensions—stripped bare of everything but a humble and passionately seeking *heart*. He says to the soul, "Long for Me, and I will show Myself. Desire Me with a great desire, and I will be found."

Scattered all through history are innumerable persons, both great and insignificant, who looked for the Pearl of Great Price: and not too many would seem to have found it. Some sought by study, by intelligence; some by strict and pious attention to outward ceremonial service; some by a "religious" life; some even by penance and fasting. Those who found sought with the heart. Those who sought with careful piety, or with intelligence, found perhaps faith and submission, but no joy. The Pearl is that which cannot be described in words. It is the *touch of God Himself upon the soul*, the Joy of Love.

The entrance to the land of happiness and peace is through union of the will to Christ, by love. How can this sense of love be reached? By centering the wheel of the mind, with its daily spinning thoughts, upon the Man-Jesus, and learning inwardly to see and hold on to the perfect simplicity and love of Jesus Christ, we can form the habit of taking Jesus as our heart and mind companion. We are all aware of the unceasing necessity of the mind to fill itself: we cannot have *no* thoughts until we have advanced in the spiritual life to a long distance. We may well see, in this, one of the provisions made by God for His own habitation in the mind of man—a habitation too often hideously usurped by every kind of unworthy substitute. Petty social interests and occupations, personal animosities, ambitions, worries, a revolving endless chaos of futilities, known and praised by too many of us as "a busy life"!—the mind being given opportunity only at long intervals, and usually at stated and set times, to dwell upon the thought of God, and the marvelous future of the human spirit. We are like travelers who, about to start out upon a great journey, pack their portmanteaux with everything that will be *perfectly useless to them!*

Now, it is possible to put out and obliterate this chaotic and useless state of mind, which would appear to be the "natural mind," and to open ourselves to receive the might and force and the joys and delights of Christ's Mind. These joys are the Heart of Christ speaking to the heart of His lover. They are incomparable: beyond all imagination until we know them; and we receive them and perceive them and enjoy them as we have largeness and capacity to contain them. For there is no end. He has ever more to give if we will be but large enough to receive.

Is baptism of itself sufficient to get us into this Kingdom? No. Is the leading of an orderly social life sufficient to find it? No. Is the hope, even the earnest expectation, that we shall, by some means or other (we do not know by what!), be brought to it, sufficient to find it? No; not without the *personal laying hold* can we ever achieve it. Shall we find it in much outward study? No; and our aim is, not to be the student but the possessor; and the key to this possession is not in books, but, for us, in Jesus. He it is who must be invited and admitted into the heart with great tenderness—with all those virtues for which He stands—and made the center point of thought. Out of constant thought grows tenderness; out of tenderness, affection; out of affection, love. Love once firmly fixed in the heart for Jesus, we get a perception (by contrast) of our own faults—very painful, and known as repentance. This should be succeeded at once by change of mind, i.e. we try to push out the old way of thinking and acting and take on a new way. We try, in fact, strenuously to please the Beloved, to be in harmony with Him; and now we have established a personal relationship between ourselves and Christ.

With the perception of our own failings comes the necessary humility and the drastic elimination of all prides. We remember, too, that although Jesus is so near to us, and our own Beloved, He is also the mighty Son of God. He is also the mystical Christ, who, when we are ready, leads us to the Father: which is to say, that we are suddenly stricken with the consciousness of and the love for God; and here we enter that most wonderful of all earthly experiences—the Soul's great Garden of Happiness.

To be a student of theories, dogmas, laws, and writings of men is to be involved in endless controversy; and we may study books till we are sick, and embrace nothing but vapor for all our pains. To be a pupil and possessor we must first establish the personal relationship between ourselves and Jesus. To do this we must realize more fully than we now do that He *still lives*. The mind is inclined to dwell on Him mostly as *having lived*. When we have taught ourselves to realize that Jesus is as intensely alive to everything that we do as He was when He visibly walked with men—that Jesus is as easily aware of our inmost thoughts and endeavors now as He was of the secret thoughts of His disciples—then we shall have brought Him much closer into our own life.

To Be Wholly Pleasing to Him
We often think. Where am I at fault? I am unable to *see* myself as a sinner, though publicly I confess myself to be one. For I keep the commandments; I am friendly to my neighbors; I am just to my fellowmen; I can think of no particular harm that I do. Why, then, am I a sinner? And our very modesty and reverence may forbid us to compare ourselves with God. Yet here lies our mistake; for if we would enter the Garden of Happiness and Peace, which is the Kingdom of God, this is the commencement of our advance—that we should compare ourselves in all things with God, in whose likeness we are made, and, making such full observation as we are able of the terrible gulfs between ourselves and Him, should with tears and humility and

constant endeavor be at great pains and stress to make good to Him our deficiencies.

"Be ye perfect as I am perfect."

"Be ye holy as I am holy."

If this were not attainable, He would not have set so high a goal. In this, then, we are sinners—that we are not pure and lovely as God Himself! This is a prodigious, an almost unthinkable, height; yet He wills us to attempt it, and all the powers of Heaven are with us as we climb.

Though on reading the Gospels carefully we may be unable to come to any other conclusion than that Jesus Christ neither prayed for nor died for all mankind, but only for the elect, yet we see equally clearly that all mankind is *invited to be the elect.* We are, then, not individually sure of Heaven because Jesus died upon a cross for men; but sure of Heaven for ourselves only if we individually will to live and think and act in such a manner that *we become of the elect.* "Him that cometh to Me I will in no wise cast out," says the Voice of the Beloved.

In our early stages, how we shrink from the mere word, or idea, of perfection; and later, what we would give to be able to achieve it! Yet though we shrink so from the thought of it, we know instinctively that we must try to approach it; if we would stay near Him, we must be wholly pleasing to Him. We think of saints—we know nothing of saints, but think of them as most unusual persons midway between men and angels, and know ourselves not fashioned for any such position: and how change ourselves, how alter our character, as grown men and women? It is Christ who can show us the way.

The Water of Life is the Mind of Christ, and the true object of life is to learn how to receive this Mind of Christ: for by it and with it we enter the Kingdom of God. And how shall we receive the Mind of Christ? Here is our difficulty. Firstly, we may do it through sympathy with, and a drawing near to, the Man-Jesus, accompanied by such drastic changes of mind as we are able to accomplish *to show our goodwill.* We may learn to become more unselfish, more patient, more sympathetic to others, and to curb the tongue, so that words which are untrue or unkind shall not slip off it. We can learn to govern the animal that is in us, instead of being governed by it.

And next, having become well knitted to the Man-Jesus, the Christ will draw us forward step by step through all the next inward stages, we giving to Him our attention; and He will bring us finally to that marvelous condition of God-consciousness by which He is able perpetually to refresh and renew us. There is one great first rule to hold to, which is *to think lovingly of Jesus*: in this way we eventually and automatically *come into a state of love*. In which state He will teach us to put out our own little light, that we may learn to live by the lovely light of God. And we have entered the Kingdom!

The Sparkle of God

We confuse in our minds the two separate essences—that of the soul and that of the human spirit (heart, intelligence, and will), which are widely different; the soul acting for us as the wings of the creature. And above and superior to the soul, and yet within it, is the divine and incorruptible Spirit or Sparkle of God, which in its turn acts as the wings of the soul. So we have the worm (or creature-spirit), the soul; and the Celestial Spark, or Divine Intelligence of the soul, which is the organ of God, and with which we are able to come in *sensible contact* with the divine world and God Himself. What are our enemies? Selfishness, impatience, covetousness, pride, ill-temper, bodily indulgences, and, above all, indifference to God of the will of the creature.

Some men say that man has invented for himself the thought of God, because of the great need he feels within himself for such a being. Yet look where we will in Nature, do we find a warrant for such a thought? Are babes inspired with the desire for milk, and is that milk withheld from the nature of all mothers? No; to the babe is given the desire because the mother has where-with to satisfy. So with grown men: for to us is given a deep and secret desire for the milk of God's love, and to Himself He has reserved the joy of leading us to it and bestowing it upon us.*

---

* Editor's Note: Staveley goes on to speak of her early life and her relationship first with the Man-Jesus, then with Jesus-as-Christ, then with the Godhead. This section has been omitted as readers of this anthology should already be familiar with Staveley's life story from *The Prodigal Returns*.

The Remedy of Prayer

Sometimes for a short while the soul will suffer from a sickness (I speak now for persons already very well advanced); she is parched and without sweetness. Her love has no joy in it. This is not a condition to be accepted or acquiesced in, but must be overcome at once by a remedy of prayer: prayer addressed to the Father, *in the name of Jesus Christ*, a prayer of praise and adoration—"I praise and bless and love and thank Thee, I praise and bless and love and worship Thee, I praise and bless and love and glorify Thee"—till the heart is fired and we return to the intimacy of love. Or the Lord's Prayer, very slow, and with an intention both outgoing and *intaking*. So far I have never known these remedies to fail, and joy floods the soul and sends her swinging up, up on to the topmost heights again. It is magnificent.

How is it that we can pass so, up from the visible into the Invisible, and become so one with it, and feel it so powerfully, that the Invisible becomes a thousand times more real to us than the visible! It is like a different manner of living altogether. And when anyone so living finds himself even for a short time unfastened from this way of living and back again to what is known to the average as normal life, this normal life seems no better to him than some horrible chaotic and uneven turmoil. When so unfastened, the whole savor of life is completely gone, and a smallness of mind and outlook is fallen back into, from which the soul recoils in horror and struggles quickly to free herself.

Is this the remnant of the unruly creature rising up and grappling with the soul again? Is this some deliberate trial of us by the Master?—or some natural spiritual sickness? Whilst in this condition we must disappoint the Beloved. On the other hand, we find ourselves kept to the knowledge of our own impotence and dependence, and the spirit is strengthened by the efforts made quickly to recover the lost beautiful estate. Also we become more able to feel true patience and compassion for such others as do not know the way of escape. So we gain, maybe, more than we lose.

We may wonder how it is that the Mighty Maker of the Universe should choose to condescend to the mere individual piece of clay. It is incomprehensible. It is so incomprehensible that there is but one way of looking at it. This is no favoritism to the individual, but the evidence of a Mind with a vast plan pursuing a way and using a likely individual. These individuals or willing souls He takes and, setting them apart, fashions them to His own ends and liking. Of one He will make a worker, and of another He fashions to Himself a lover. It would seem to be His will to use the human implement to help the human. As water, for usefulness to the many, must be collected and put through channels, so it would seem must the beneficence of God be collected into human vessels and channels that it may be distributed for the use of the many and the more feeble.

Why Mortify the Body?
Why mortify the body with harsh austerities? When we over-mortify the body with fastings, pains, and penances we are *remembering the flesh*. Let us aim at the forgetting and not the despising of the flesh. A sick body can be a great hindrance to the soul. By keeping the body in a state of perfect wholesomeness we can more easily pass away from the recollection of it. Chastise the mind rather than the body. Christ taught, not the contempt or willful neglect of the body, but the humble submission of the body to all *circumstances*, the obedience of the will to God, and the glorious and immeasurable possibilities of the human spirit.

God Contact
We know that the love of the heart can be beautiful and full of zeal and fervor; but the love of the soul by comparison to it is like a furnace, and the capacities of the heart are not worthy to be named in the same breath. Yet, deplorable as is the heart of man, it is evidently desired by God, and must be given to Him before He will waken the soul. To my belief, we are quite unable to awaken our own soul, though we are able to *will* to love God with the heart, and through this we pass up to the border of the Veil of Separation, where He will *sting the soul into life* and we have Perception.

After which the soul will often be swept or plucked up into immeasurable glories and delights which are neither imagined nor contrived, nor even desired by her at first—for how can we desire that which we have never heard of and cannot even imagine? And these delights are unimaginable before the soul is caught up into them, and to my experience they constantly differ. The soul knows herself to be in the hands and the power of another, outside herself. She does not enter these joys of her own power or of her own will, but by permission and intention and will of a force outside herself though perceived and known inside herself.

How can a Contact with God be in any way described? It is not seeing, but meeting and fusion with awareness. The soul retaining her own individuality and consciousness to an intense degree, but imbued with and fused into a life of incredible intensity, which passes through the soul vitalities and emotions of a life so new, so vivid, so amazing, that she knows not whether she has been embraced by love or by fire, by joy or by anguish: for so fearful is her joy that she is almost unable to endure the might of it.

And how can the heat or fire of God be described? It is very far from being like the cruelty of fire, and yet it is so tremendous that the mind knows of little else to compare it to. But it is like a vibration of great speed and heat, like a fluid and magnetic heat. This heat is of many degrees and of several kinds. The heat of Christ is mixed with indescribable sweetness: giving marvelous pleasure and refreshment and happiness, and wonderfully adapted to the delicacy of the human creature. The heat of the Godhead is very different, and sometimes we may even feel it to be cruel and remorseless in its very terrible and swift intensity. But the soul, like all great lovers, never flinches or hangs back, but passionately lends herself. If He chose to kill her with this joy she would gladly have it so.

On Rapture and Ecstasy

There is another manner. The Spirit comes upon the soul in waves of terrible power. Now in a rapture God descends upon the soul, catching her suddenly up in a marvelous embrace: magnetizing her, ravishing her. He is come, and He is gone. In an ecstasy the soul goes out prepared to meet Him, seeking Him by praise and prayer, pouring up her love towards Him; and He, condescending to her, fills her with unspeakable delights, and at rare times He will catch her from an ecstasy into a greater rapture. At least, so it is with me: the ecstasy is prepared for, but in the quicker rapture (or catching up) it is He that seeks the soul. These two conditions, though given very intermittently, become a completely natural experience. I should say that the soul lived by this way: it is her food and her life, which she receives with all the simplicity and naturalness of the hungry man turning to his bodily food. But these waves of power were something altogether new and very hard to endure. As each wave passed I would come up out of it, as it were, gasping. It was as if something too great for the soul to contain was being forced through her. It was as if one should try to force at fearful pressure fluid through a body too solid to be percolated by it. I understood nothing of what could be intended by such happenings, neither could I give accommodation to this intensity.

I tried to make myself a wholly willing receptacle and instrument, but after the third day of this I could not bear any more. I was greatly distressed. I could not understand what was required of me. I gave myself totally to Him, and it was not enough. And at last I cried to Him, saying: "I understand nothing: forgive me, my God, for my great foolishness, but Thy power is too much for me. Do what Thou wilt with me; I am altogether Thine. Drown me with Thy strength, break me in pieces—I am willing; only do it quickly, my Lord, and have done with it, for I am so small. But I love Thee with all that I have or am; yet I am overwhelmed: I am still too little to be taught in this way, it is too much for my strength. Yet do as Thou wilt; I love Thee, I love Thee." And He heard me, and He ceased: and He returned to the ways that I understood and dearly loved, and for weeks I lived in Paradise. But my body was dreadfully shaken, and I suffered with my heart and breathing.

Shortly after I began to know that another change had come into me. God had become intensely my Father, and Christ the lover was gone up again into the Godhead—as happened after my third conversion upon the hill. So great, so tremendous was this sense of the *Fatherhood* of God become that I had only to think the word Father to seem to be instantly transported into His very bosom. Oh, the mighty sweetness of it! But it is not an ecstasy. The creature and soul are dead to world-life, as in a rapture or ecstasy; but the soul is not the bride, she is the child, and, full of eager and adoring intimacy, she flies into His ever-open arms, and never, never does she miss the way. Oh, the sweetness of it, the great, great glory of it, and the folly of words! If only all the world of men and women could have this joy! How to help even one soul towards it is what fills my heart and mind. How convince them, how induce them to take the first steps? It is the first steps we need to take. He does not drive, He calls. "Come to Me," He calls. It is this failure to have the will to go to Him which is the root of all human woe. Would we but take the first few steps towards Him, He will carry us all the rest of the way. These first few steps we take holding to the hand of Jesus. For the so-called Christian there is no other way (but he is no Christian until he has taken it). For the

Buddhist, doubtless, Gautama is permitted to do the same. But for those who are baptized in Jesus Christ's name, He is their only Way.

Never Despise Creation

O marvelous and exquisite God! I am so enraptured by Thy nearness, I am so filled with love and joy, that there is no one, nothing, in heaven or earth to me save Thine Own Self, and I could die for love of Thee! Indeed I am in deep necessity to find Thee at each moment of the day, for so great is Thy glamour that without Thee my days are like bitter waters and a mouthful of gravel to a hungry man. How long wilt Thou leave me here—set down upon the earth in this martyrdom of languishing for love of Thee? And suddenly, when the pain can be endured no more, He embraces the soul. Then where do sorrow and waiting fly?—and what is pain? There never were such things!

I find the lark the most wonderful of all birds. I cannot listen to his rhapsodies without being inspired (no matter what I may be in the midst of doing or saying) to throw up my own love to God. In the soaring insistence of his song and passion I find the only thing in Nature which so suggests the high-soaring and rapturous flights of the soul. But I am glad that we surpass the lark in sustaining a far more lengthy and wonderful flight; and that we sing, not downwards to an earthly love, but upwards to a heavenly.

To my mind, this is man's only justification for considering himself above the beasts—that we can love, and communicate with, God. For where otherwise is his superiority? He builds fine buildings which crumble and decay. He digs holes in the earth to take out treasures which he has not made; and if he makes himself the very highest tower of wealth or fame, he must come down from it and be buried in the earth like any other carcass.

It is better not to contend, either with others or against our own body. If we contend against anything we impress it the more firmly upon our consciousness. So if we would overcome the lusts of the body, let us do it not by harming or by contending against the body, which but emphasizes its powers and importance, but let us rather proceed to ignore and make little of the body by forgetting it and passing out of it into higher things; and eventually we shall learn to live, not in the lower state, but in the joy of the soul. Why have a contempt for the body? I once did, and found that I was committing a great sin against the Maker of it. How dare we say "my body is vile," when He fashioned it! It is blasphemous, when we consider that it is His Temple.

To my mind the body is a beautiful and wonderful thing, and is greatly sinned against by our evil hearts and minds and tongues. The body would do no harm if we, with our free-will, did not think out the wickedness first in our own hearts. For first we commit theft and adultery with the mind, and then we cause the body to carry out these things. We know that the body is under the law, and its appetites are under the law, but the heart and mind and tongue are perpetual breakers of this law. It is lawful for the body to take its meat and drink, but not to be surfeited and drunken. It is lawful for the body to have its desires and its loves, but not to be promiscuous and unfaithful. But we know that a better way is to turn all appetites and greeds to this; that we be greedy and ravenous for Christ. Only so shall we use the appetites of mind and heart and body for their true end, and that not by despising but by conversion.

With great insistence I have been taught not to despise anything whatever in Creation of *things made* in His most beautiful and wonderful world, though often I may cry with tears, "Lord God! raise me to a world holier and nearer to Thyself, for I am heartbroken here." Yet I am taught only to despise such things as lying, deceitfulness, hypocrisy, and uncleanness—in fact, stenches of the heart and mind—and not to think too much about these, but, passing on, drop out the recollection of them in thoughts of finer things.

The Withdrawal of Grace

Is the temporary loss of grace our fault, or is it a deliberate withdrawal and testing upon His part? Both. Every condition that we are in which is not pure and perfect of its kind, such as pure peace, pure joy, pure harmony, is because of failure on our part to *hold* to Him. Whenever, and for so long, as we keep ourselves in the single and simple condition of mind and heart necessary for the perception and reception of Him, for just so long shall we receive and perceive him; but this condition again we cannot maintain without grace. All loss of joy, of serenity, of contact, is failure, then, on our part or withdrawal upon His. Yet we learn a bitter but useful lesson by these losses of ability for connection. To return ignominiously to our dust is a most bitter humiliation and trial—indeed, a desolation. Now, if we did not so return we might suppose ourselves able, of our own power, not only to achieve momentary connection with the Divine, but to remain at will in this sublime condition, by which I mean in a state bordering upon ecstasy. The withdrawal of grace therefore would seem to be a necessary part of the education and of the constant humbling of the soul. To find ourselves, of our own unaided capacity, by the mere force of our own will, able constantly to go up to so high a level would inevitably foster pride; indeed, to attain such a capacity would seem to place us on a level with the angels!

For the carrying out of His plan, it would seem to be His good pleasure that we are just what we are—not angels, but little human things, full of simplicity and trust and love. "Like dear children," as St Paul says; and yet, oh! wonder of wonders! *far more than this.* For whilst we patiently wait, from time to time He stoops and embraces the soul in an infinite bliss, in which we are no more children, but are caught up into High Love.

It is hard to conquer in small things, petty irritations, worries, cares of this world, likes and dislikes—all of these being subtle temptations, and all selfish. For instance, very often I find the human voice the most horrible thing that I know! I will be in a beautiful state of mind, and people around me will drag me from it with their maddening inanities of conversation. This one will speak of the weather, and that one of food; another of scandal, another of amusements. They will talk of their love for a dog, for a horse, for golf, for men or women; but never do I hear at any time, or anywhere, anyone speak of their love for God. I must listen to all their loves, but if I should venture to speak of mine they would look at me amazed; indeed, I never should dare to do it. And this is perhaps the greatest weakness that I have to fight against now, and one that spoils the harmony of the mind more than any other—that I cannot always control myself from secret though unspoken irritation, impatience, and criticisms.

And every such failure is a disappointment to the Beloved. Many times I say to Him, "What canst Thou do with us all, Beloved—such a mass of selfish, foolish, blundering, sinful creatures, all hanging and pulling on to Thee at the same moment?" And I will be filled with a passionate desire to so progress that I may stand a little alone and not be a perpetual drag upon Him, and, feeling strong, perhaps I will say: "I will give up my share of Thee to someone else, and not draw upon Thee for a little while, my Beloved Lord." But oh, in less than an hour, if He should take me at my word! I could cry and moan like a small child, in my horrible emptiness and longing for Him. And where now is my strength?—I have not an ounce of it without Him! By this I learn in my own person how He is life itself to us, in all ways. He is the air, the bread, and the blood of the soul, and no one can live without at every moment drawing upon Him, though they do it insensibly. What a weight to carry, what a burden, this whole hungry clamoring mass of disobedient men and women! Oh, my Beloved, how frequently I weep for all Thy bitter disappointment—never ending!

But this we may be sure of—that all the marvels of His grace are not poured out on some poor scrap-pit for no other reason than to give him pleasure. There is a vast purpose behind it all, and by keenest attention we must pick up this purpose, understand it, *and do it*. This is the true work of man, to love God with all the heart and mind and soul and strength, and not those material works with which we all so easily satisfy ourselves and our consciences, and our *bodily* needs.

The Locality of the Soul

God has marvelous ways (and very difficult to the beginner) of conveying His wishes. To my finding, the inward life of us is like a perpetual interchange of conversation between the heart and its many desires and the mind (which for myself I put into three parts—the intelligence, the will, the reason). Now, all these parts of my heart and of my mind formerly occupied themselves entirely with worldly things, passing from one thing to another in most disorderly fashion; but now they occupy themselves (save for bodily necessities) *solely* with Him. There is a perpetual smooth and beautiful conversation between them *to* Him and *of* Him; and suddenly He will seem to enter into this conversation, suggesting thoughts which are not mine.

I do not remember when I first became fully conscious that the center or seat of my emotions was changed, and that I now responded to all the experiences of life only with the higher parts of me. This change I found inexplicable and remarkable, for it was fundamental, and yet neither intended nor thought of by me. With this alteration in the physical correspondences to life came a corresponding alteration in the spiritual part of me.

Formerly I supposed that the soul dwelt in, or was even a part of, the mind. Now, though the mind must be filled wholly with God, and all other things whatsoever put out of it if we would contemplate Him or respond to Him, yet neither the brain nor the intelligence of the creature can come into any contact with Him; and this I soon learnt. Correspondence with the Divine is accomplished for the creature through the heart and by the uppermost part of the breast, this latter place (above the heart and below the mind) is the dwelling-place of the celestial spark of the soul, which lies, as it were, between two fires—that of the heart and that of the mind, responding directly to neither of these, but to God only.

Before I was touched upon the hill I was not aware of the locality of any part of my soul, neither was there anything which could convince me that I even possessed a soul. I did no more than believe and suppose that I did possess one. But the soul, once revived, becomes the most powerful and vivid part of our being; we are not able any longer to mistake its possession or position in the body. She is indeed the wonderful and lovely mistress of us, with which alone we can unlock the mysteries of God's love.

How poor and cold a thing is mere belief! No longer do I *believe* in Jesus Christ: I do *possess him.* So complete is the change that He brings about in us that I now only count my life and my time from the first day of this new God-consciousness that I received upon the hill, for that was the first day of my real life; just as formerly I would count my time from the first day of my physical birth, and from that on to my falling in love and to my marriage, which once seemed to me to be the most important dates.

Whilst these changes were taking place in me I would often be filled with uneasiness and some alarm; asking myself what all this could mean and if it could be the way of martyrs or saints, for I had no courage or liking to be one or the other and was very frightened of suffering. And I think my cunning heart would have liked to take all the sweets and leave the bitter. How well He knew this, and how exquisitely He handled me, never forcing, only looking at me, *inviting* me with those marvelous perfections of His! How could I possibly resist Him? All the while, all my waking hours, I felt that strange, new, incomprehensible, steady, insistent *drawing* and urgency of the Spirit in me. Little by little I went—and still go—*towards* perfection, whilst my cowardly heart endured many fears.

It was not any desire for my own salvation; to this I have never given so much as two thoughts. It was the *irresistible attraction* of our marvelous and beautiful God. He lured, He drew me with His loveliness, His holy perfections, His unutterable purity. *I longed to please*

Him. The whole earth was filled with the glamour of Him, and I filled with horror to see how utterly unlike—apart from the glorious Beloved—I was. How frightful my blemishes, which must stink in His nostrils! Think of it! To stink in the nostrils of the Beloved! What lover could endure to do such a thing? No effort could be too great or painful to beautify oneself for Him. In this there is no virtue; it is the driving necessity of love, a necessity known by every lover worthy of the name on earth. To please and obey this ineffable and exquisite Being!—the privilege intoxicated me more and more.

Our greatest need is to relearn the will of God. For we are so separated from Him that we now look upon His Will as on a cross, as an incomprehensible sacrifice, as but self abnegation, pain, and gloom. We repudiate it in terror. If we have the will to relearn His Will, we stand still and think of it, we walk to seek it, we try to accept it, trembling we bow down to it with obedience and many tears; and behold! it changes to an Invitation, a sigh of beauty, a breath of spring, the song of birds, the faces of flowers, the ever-ascending spiral of the mating of all loves, the sunshine of the Universe; and at last, intoxicated with happiness, we say: "My God, my Love, I sip and drink Thy Will as an ambrosial Wine!"

On the Sacrament of Marriage

To the lover of God all affections go up and become enclosed, as it were, into one affection which is Himself; so that we have no love for anyone or anything *apart* from Him. In this is included, in a most deep and mysterious fashion, marriage-love in all its aspects. In every way it can become a sacrament: there is nothing in it which is not holy, in no way does the marriage bond of the body separate the spirit from acceptableness to God.

But I was some time before I could arrive at this, and could see marriage as the physical prototype in this physical world of the spiritual union with Himself in the spiritual world. And this was arrived at, not by prudish questionings and criticisms, but by remembering that this relationship between men and women is His thought, His plan, not ours. We are responsible for our part in it only in so far as to keep the bond of it pure and clean and sweet, and submit ourselves in all things as *completely and orderly as possible to His plans, whatever they may be*. In this attitude of unquestioning, unresisting submission, the Holy Spirit finds a swift and easy channel through us. It is our opposition to the passage of the Holy Will which causes all the distress and uneasiness of life. He has no wish to impose distress and suffering upon us. His Will towards us is pure joy, pure love, pure peace, pure sweetness. This bond of earthly marriage is of the flesh and can be kept by the body, and yet the heart, mind, and soul remain in lovely perfect chastity; and I found that this exquisite freedom—after prolonged endeavors on the part of the soul and the creature—was at length given them as a gift by act of grace, and remained in permanence without variation.

The Road of Love
The more I see of and talk with other people, the more I see how greatly changed I am. I am *freed*. They are bound. I find them bound by fears, by anxieties, by worries, by apprehensions of evil things, by sadness, by fears of death for their loved ones or for themselves. Now, we are freed of all these things *if we keep to the Way*, which is the Road of Love. This change we do not bring about for ourselves, and do not perhaps even realize that it can be effected. For myself, I seemed to be lifted into it, or into a *capacity* for it, on that day and in that moment in which I first loved God. This is not to say that since that moment I have not had to struggle, suffer, and endure, to keep myself in, and progress in this condition; but my sufferings, struggles, and endurances, being for love and in love and because of love, were and are in themselves beautiful, and leave in the recollection nothing inharmonious. They are the difficult prelude to a glorious melody.

Another thing—we become by this love for Him so large that we seem to embrace within our own self the Universe! In some mysterious manner we become in sympathy with all things in the bond of His making.

Are these things worth nothing whatever, that the majority of people should be content to spend their lives looking for five-pound notes and even shillings and this not only the poor, but the rich more so? I am far more at a loss to understand my fellow-men than I am to understand God. We have need of the shillings, but of other and more lovely things besides, which cost no money and may be had by the poorest. It is rapidly becoming the only sorrow of my life that people do not all come to share this Life in which I live. How that parable knocks at the heart, "Go out into the high-ways and the hedges and compel them to come in!" To know all this *fullness* of life and not to be able to bring even my nearest and dearest into it: what a terrible mystery is this!—it is an agony. Now, in this agony I share the Agony of Jesus. This is a part of the Cross, and only the Father can make it straight. I see Heaven held out, and *refused*; love held out, and *refused*; perfection shown, and killed upon a cross. What is the crucifix but that most awful of all things—the Grief of God made Visible? Perfect Love submitting itself to the vile freewill of man and dying of wounds!

The Joy of Adoration

As we progress in this new way of living we find an increasing difficulty in maintaining petition; for on commencing to petition we will almost invariably be instantly lifted up to such a state of adoration that the whole soul is nothing but a burning song, a thing of living worship. At first I was inclined to blame myself, but now I know that it is acceptable for us to pass from petitioning (no matter who or what for) to high adoration, even though it is a great personal indulgence (and the petitioning is a *hard task*)—an indulgence so extreme that I cannot call to my mind anything in any experience or time of my life, excepting actual raptures, which could, or can, in any way compare or be named in the same breath with this most marvelous joy; for out of this joy of adoration flows the Song of the Soul.

And all these previous years of my life I have lived with the greater part of me dead, and most persons the same! The more I think of it, the more amazed I am at our folly—working and fretting, and striving and looking for every kind of thing except the one thing, beautiful, needful, and living, which is the finding of the personal connection between ourselves and God and the Waters of Life.

On Passive and Active Contemplation

The contemplation of God might be expressed as the folding up or complete forgetfulness of all earthly and bodily things, desires, and attractions, and the raising of the heart and mind and the centering of them in great and joyful intensity upon God, by means of love. Of this contemplation of God I find two principal forms: the passive and the active. In the first we are in a state of steady, quiet, and loving perception and reception, and at some farness; in this we are able to remain for hours, entering this state when waking at dawn and remaining in it till rising.

In active contemplation we are in rapturous and passionate adoration with great nearness, and are not able to remain in it long because of bodily weakness. The soul feels to be never tired by the longest flight, but must return because of the exhaustion of the forlorn and wretched creature, which creature is complete in itself, having its body, of which, being able to touch it, we say, "It is my body," and its heart and mind with intelligence, of which we are wont to think, "This is myself"; yet it is but a part, for the intelligence of our creature is by no means the intelligence of the divine soul, but a far lesser light: for with the intelligence of the divine soul we reach out to God and attain Him, but with the intelligence of the creature we reach towards Him but do not attain, for with it we are unable to penetrate the veil. Therefore, who would know the joys of contemplation must come to them by love, for love is the only means by which the creature can attain. The soul attains God as her birthright, but the creature by adoption and redemption, and this through love. By love the creature dies and is reborn into the spirit.

Singleness of Heart
The word "poverty," as used to express a necessary condition of our coming to God, is a most misleading term. For how can any condition be rightly named poverty which brings us into the riches of God? Rather let us use the words "singleness of heart," or "simplicity": which is to say, we *put out* all other interests save those pleasing to God (to commence with), and afterwards we reach the condition in which we *have no* interests but in God Himself—the heart and mind and will of the creature becoming wholly God's, and God filling them. How can we say, then, that it is poverty to be filled with God! Rather is it rightly expressed as being a heart fixed in singleness upon God, through drastic simplification of interests: the which is no poverty, but the wealth of all the Universe.

Contemplation of Nature
Lately I have seen the word "contemplation" used as expressing the heights of attainment in God-consciousness of men, and I find it inadequate. From the age of seventeen I fell into the habit of contemplation, not of God, but of Nature: which is to say, I would first place myself, sitting, in such a position that my body would not fall and I might completely forget it, and then would look about me and drink

in the beauty of the scene, my eyes coming finally to rest upon the spot most beautiful to me. There they remained fixed. All thoughts were now folded up so that my mind, flowing singly in one direction, concentrated itself upon the beauty on which I gazed. This soon vanished, and I saw nothing whatever, but, bearing away into a place of complete silence and emptiness, I there assimilated and enjoyed inwardly the soaring essence of the beauty which I had previously drawn into my mind through my eyes, being now no longer conscious of seeing outwardly, but living entirely from the inward.

This I did almost every day, but to do it I was obliged to seek solitude, and absolute solitude is a hard thing to find; but I sought it, no matter where, even in a churchyard! I saw no graves. I saw the sky, or a marvelous cloud pink with the kisses of the sun, and away I went. I judge this now to have been contemplation, though I never thought of it by so fine-sounding a name; it was only my delightful pastime, yet there was a strange inexpressible sadness in it. Nature and beauty were not enough. The more beauty I saw, the more I longed for something to which I could not put a name. At times the ache of this pain became terrible, almost agonizing, but I could not forgo my pastime. Now, at last, I know what this pain was: my soul looked for God, but my creature did not know it. For just in this same way we contemplate God, savoring Him without seeing Him, and being filled to the brim with marvelous delights with no sadness.

But this condition of contemplation is very far from being the mountain-top; it is but a high plateau from which we make the final ascent. The summit is an indescribable contact, and this summit is not one summit but many summits. Which is to say, we have contact of several separate forms—that of giving, that of receiving, and that of immersion or absorption, which *at its highest* is altogether unendurable as fire.

Of this last I am able only to say this: that not only is it inexpressible by any words, but that that which is a state of extreme beatitude to the soul is death to the creature by excess of joy. Therefore both heart and mind fear to recall any details of the memory of this highest attainment. I knew it but once. To know it again would be the death of my body. For more than two hours (as well as I am able to judge) before becoming to this highest experience, my soul traveled through what felt to be an ocean, for she rose and fell upon billows in a state of infinite bliss.

Of other forms of contact we have a swift, unexpected, even unsought for attainment, which is entirely of His volition; that sudden condescension to the soul, in which in unspeakable rapture she is caught up to her holy lover.

These are the topmost heights which the creature dare recall, though to the soul they remain in memory as life itself. The variations of these forms of contact are infinite, for God would seem to will to be both eternal changelessness and variation in infinitude. But to my feeling all degrees of attainment are only to be distinguished as varying degrees of union, the joy of which is of a form and a degree of intensity and purity which can enter neither the heart nor the mind to imagine, but must be experienced to be understood, and when experienced remains in part incomprehensible. It is not to be obtained by force of the will, neither can it be obtained without the will. It is, then, a mystery of two wills in unison, in which our will is temporarily fused into and consumed by the will of God and is in transports of felicity over its own annihilation! This is outside reason and therefore incomprehensible to the creature, but comprehensible to the soul, and becomes the aim and object of our life to attain in permanence, and is the uttermost limit of all conceivable rapture.

Beloved, Thou takest the creature and liftest it up; Thou takest the creature and liftest it high, so that nevermore can it offend Thee, and the soul is free to sing of her love. Then is it Thy will that the creature should love Thee? Or is it Thy will that the soul should adore? Beloved, I know not whether with my heart and mind I most adore Thee, or whether with my soul I love Thee more. And where is that secret trysting-place of love? I do not know; for whilst I go there and whilst I return I am blind, and whilst I am there I am blinded by Love Himself. O wondrous trysting-place! which is indeed the only trysting-place of all the world worthy to be named.

The Mantle of God-Consciousness
As the loving creature progresses he will find himself ceasing to live in things, or thoughts of things or of persons, but his whole mind and heart will be concentrated upon the thought of God alone. Now Jesus, now the High Christ, now the Father, but never away from one of the aspects or personalities of God, though his conditions of nearness will vary. For at times he will be in a condition of great nearness, at times in a condition of some farness, or, more properly speaking, of

obscurity. He will be in a condition of waiting (this exceedingly frequent, the most frequent of all); a condition of amazing happiness; a condition of pain, of desolation at being still upon the earth instead of with God. He will be in a condition of giving love to God, or a condition of receiving love, of remembrance and attention. He will be in a condition of immeasurable glamour, an extraordinary illumination of every faculty, not by any act of his own, but poured through him until he is filled with the elixir of some new form of life, and feels himself before these experiences never to have lived—he but existed as a part of Nature. But now, although he is become more united to Nature than ever before, he also is mysteriously drawn apart from her; without being in any way presumptuous, he feels to be above her, not by any merits but by intention of Another. He is become lifted up into the spirit and essence of Nature, and the heavy and more obvious parts of her bind him no more. He is in a condition of freedom, he is frequently in a condition of great splendor, and is wrapped perpetually round about with that most glorious mantle—God-consciousness.

For the truly loving soul here on earth there are no longer heavens, nor conditions of heavens, nor grades, nor crowns, nor angels, nor archangels, nor saints, nor holy spirits; but, going out and up and on, we reach at last THE ONE, and for marvelous unspeakably glorious moments KNOW HIM.

Flights of the Soul
These beautiful flights of the soul cannot be taken through idleness, though they are taken in what would outwardly appear to be a great stillness. This stillness is but the necessary abstraction from physical activity, even from physical consciousness; but inwardly the spirit is in a great activity, a very ferment of secret work. This, to the writer, is frequently produced by the beautiful in Nature, the spirit involuntarily passing at the sight of beauty into a passionate admiration for the Maker of it. This high, pure emotion, which is also an *intense activity* of the spirit, would seem so to etherealize the creature that instantly the delicate soul is able to escape her loosened bonds and flies towards her home, filled with ineffable, incomparable delight, praising, singing, and joying in her Lord and God until the body can endure no more, and swiftly she must return to bondage in it. But the most wonderful flights of the soul are made during a high adoring contemplation of God. We are in high contemplation when the heart,

mind, and soul, having dropped consciousness of all earthly matters, have been brought to a full concentration upon God—God totally invisible, totally unimaged, *and yet focused to a center-point by the great power of love.* The soul, whilst she is able to maintain this most difficult height of contemplation, may be visited by an intensely vivid perception, inward vision, and knowledge of God's attributes or perfections, very brief; and this *as a gift,* for she is not able to will such a felicity to herself, but being given such she is instantly consumed with adoration, and *enters ecstasy.*

Having achieved these degrees of progress, the heart and mind will say: "Now I may surely repose for I have attained!" And so we may repose, but not in idleness, which is to say, not without abundance of prayer. For only by prayer is our condition maintained and renewed; but without prayer, by which I mean an incessant inward communion, quickly our condition changes and wears away. No matter to what degree of love we have attained we need to pray for more; without persistent but short prayer for faith and love we might fall back into strange woeful periods of cold obscurity.

To the accomplished lover great and wonderful is prayer; the more completely the mind and heart are lifted up in it, the slower the wording. The greater the prayer, the shorter in words, though the longer the saying of it, for each syllable will needs be held up upon the soul before God, slowly and, as it were, in a casket of fire, and with marvelous joy. And there are prayers without words, and others without even thoughts, in which the soul in a great stillness passes up like an incense to the Most High. This is very pure, great love; wonderful, high bliss.

Method of Contemplation

The mode of entrance into active contemplation I would try to convey in this way. The body must be placed either sitting or kneeling, and supported, or flat on the back as though dead. Now the mind must commence to fold itself, closing forwards as an open rose might close her petals to a bud again, for every thought and image must be laid away and nothing left but a great forward-moving love intention. Out glides the mind all smooth and swift, and plunges deep, then takes an upward curve and up and on till willingly it faints, the creature dies, and consciousness is taken over by the soul, which, quickly coming to the trysting-place, *spreads herself* and there awaits the revelations of her God. To my feeling this final complete passing over of consciousness from the mind to the soul is by act and will of God only, and cannot be performed by will of the creature, and is the fundamental difference between the contemplation of Nature and the contemplation of God. The creature worships, but the soul alone knows contact. And yet the mode of contemplation is a far simpler thing than all these words—it is the very essence of simplicity itself; and in this sublime adventure we are really conscious of no mode nor plan nor flight, nought but the mighty need of spirit to Spirit and love to Love.

Like a Faithful Hound

The picking out and choosing of certain persons, and the naming of them "elect" and "chosen" souls, when I first read of it, filled me with such a sinking that I tried, when coming upon the words, not to admit the meaning of them into myself; for that some should be chosen and some not I felt to be favoritism, and could not understand or see the justice of it. I never asked questions. He left me in this condition for eighteen months. Then He led me to an explanation sufficient for me. The way He showed it me was not by comparisons with great things—angels and saints and holy persons; but by that humble creature, man's friend, the dog, He showed me the elect creature. It was this way.

One evening as I passed through the city I had one of those sudden strong impulses (by which He guides us) to go to a certain and particular cinematograph exhibition. I was very tired, and tried to put away the thought, but it pressed in the way that I know, and I knew it better to go. I sat for an hour seeing things that had no interest for me, and wondering why I should have had to come, when at last a film was shown of war-dogs in training—dogs trained especially to assist men and to carry their messages.

These dogs were especially selected, not for their charm of outward appearance, but for their inward capacities; *not for an especial love of the dog* (or favoritism), but for that which they were willing to learn how to do. The qualifications for (s)election were willingness, obedience, fidelity, endurance. Once chosen they were set apart. Then commenced the training, and we were shown how man put his will through the dog: he was able to do this *only because of the willingness of the dog.* The purport of the training was to carry a message for his master wherever his master willed. He must go instantly and at full speed; he must leap any obstacle; he must turn away from his own kind if they should entice him to linger on the way; he must subdue all his natural desires and instincts entirely to his master's desires; he must be indifferent to danger. And to secure this he was fired over by numbers of men, difficulties were set for him, and he was distracted from his straight course by a number of tests. Yet we saw the brave and faithful creatures running on their way at their fullest speed until, exhausted and breathless but filled with joy of *love and willingness*, they reached the journey's end, to be caressed and cared for beyond other dogs until the next occasion should arise.

Then we were shown the dog in his fully-trained condition. His master could now always rely upon him. A dog always ready, always faithful and self-forgetful, was then set apart into a still smaller and more (s)elect group and surrounded with most especial care and love. Never would it want for anything. In this there was justice. Forsaking all their natural ways, these dogs had submitted themselves wholly, in loving willingness, to their master's will, and he in return would lavish all his best on them. It was but just. Oh, how my heart leaped over it! At last I understood—for as the dog, so the human creature. We become chosen souls, not for our own sakes (which had always seemed to me such favoritism), but for our willingness to learn our Master's will. And what is His will and what is His work? Of many, many kinds, and this is shown to the soul in her training. But the hardest to learn is not that of the worker, but of the messenger and lover. As the messenger, to take His messages, in whatever direction, instantly and correctly, and to take back the answer from man to Himself—which is to say, to hold before Him the needs of man on the fire of the soul, known to most persons under the name of prayer. And as the lover, to sing to Him with never-failing joyful love and thanks.

But the learning and work of the soul is not so simple as that of the dog, who carries the message in writing upon his collar. The soul can have no written paper to assist her, and long and painful is her training; and exquisitely sweet it is when, having swiftly and accurately taken the message, she waits before Him for the rapture of those caresses that she knows so well.

How I was spurred! For I said, "Shall dogs outdo us in love and devotion?" Only in a condition of total submission, self-forgetfulness, self-abnegation, can the soul either receive or deliver her message. In this way she is justified of the joys of her election. The dog, faithful in all ways to his master, receives in return all praise and all meats, whatever he desires. The faithful soul also receives all praise and all meats, both spiritual and carnal, for nothing of earthly needs will lack her *if she asks;* and without asking, her needs are mysteriously and completely given her. Her spiritual meats are, in this world, peace, joy, ecstasy, rapture; and of the world to come it is written that eye hath not seen, nor ear heard, neither have entered into the heart of man, the things that God has prepared for them that love Him.

It might be supposed that only persons filled with public charities and social improvements, ardent and painstaking church workers, might most surely and easily learn to be messengers. But all these persons pursue and follow their own line of thought, the promptings of their own minds and hearts. They are admirable workers, but not messengers. For the hound of God must have in his heart no plan of his own. It is hard for the heart to say, "I have no wishes of my own; I have no interests, no plans, no ambitions, no schemes, no desires, no loves, no will. Thy will is my will. Thy desire is my desire. Thy love is my all. I am empty of all things, that I may be a channel for the stream of Thy will."

Our encouragements are great and extraordinary sweetnesses, urgings, and joyful uplifting of the spirit. So that when we would stop, we are pressed forward; when we are exhausted, we are filled with the wine of sweetness; when we are in tears, we are embraced into the Holy Spirit.

Sin and ill are the false notes struck by man across the harmony of God's will, and to strike upon or even remember such notes is instant banishment from the music of His presence. Where all is joy, there joy is all; and he who has not reached this joy does not know God—he is still a follower, and not a possessor, and he should refuse in his heart to remain satisfied with his condition, but climb on. Why stay behind? Climb on, climb on!

Deliverance Is Not a Burden

How often I have been mystified and disturbed by the attitude of many religious and pious people, that to follow Christ is a way of gloom, of sadness, of heaviness! How often have I gathered from sermons that we are to give up all bright and enticing things if we would follow Him, and the preacher *goes no further!* Has the Lord, then, no enticements, no sweetnesses, no brightness to offer us, that we should be asked to forsake all pleasantnesses, all brightness, all attractions, if we follow Him? This to me always seemed terrible and my heart would sink. Indeed, to my poor mind and heart it seemed nothing more hopeful than a going from bad to worse!

All the pictures I have seen, either of the Crucifixion or the Way of the Cross (and especially those of more recent times and painting), portray His Blessed Face all worn with gloom; and I know now that this is far from the truth. For perfect love knows agony, but no gloom. He went through all His agony, lifted high above gloom, in a great ecstasy of love for us.

To speak of *sacrifice* in connection with following Him, is to my mind, the work of a very foolish person and one in danger of being blasphemous. For how dare we say that it is a sacrifice when, by the putting away of foolish desires, we find God! And to find God, through the following of Jesus Christ, is to *gain so much* (even in this world, and without waiting for the next) that those who gain it never cease to be amazed at the vastness of it.

In my earlier stages I was greatly set back and disturbed by this gloom and sacrifice (which is no sacrifice) of myself so put forward by pulpit teaching. I thought I was very cowardly and sinned by this inability to like the gloomy burden, and one day I came upon this out of Jeremiah: "As for the prophet, or the priest, or the people, that shall say, The burden of the Lord, I will punish that man and his house . . . because ye say, The burden of the Lord, I will utterly forget you and forsake you, and cast you out of My presence."

These words of Jesus, "Take up thy cross and follow Me": whoever will do it will be shown by Jesus that the cross of following Him is no burden, but a deliverance, a finding of life, the way of escape, a great joy, and a garland of love. The world thinks of joyousness as being laughter, cackling, and much silly noise; and to such I do not speak. But the Christ's joyousness is of a high, still, marvelous, and ineffable completeness—beyond all words; and *wholly satisfying* to heart and soul and body and mind.

All of which is not to say that by following Him we shall escape from happenings and inconveniences and sorrows and illnesses common to life; but that when these come we are raised out of our distress into His ineffable peace. The remedy for the soul's sadness is that she should courageously pass out of her woes of exile and go up to meet her lover with smiles. Now, He cannot resist this smiling courage and love of the soul, and very quickly He must send her His sweetness, and her sadness is gone.

A New State of Innocence

When I say that if we will take a few steps alone towards Christ—which is to say, if we will make some strenuous efforts to cleanse ourselves and change our minds and ways—He will take us all the rest of the way, I speak from experience. For amongst many things this happened to me: at a certain stage, after my third conversion on the hill, He caused my former thoughts, desires, and follies to go away from me! It was as though He had sent a veil between me and such thoughts of my heart and mind as might not be pleasing to Him, so that they disappeared from my knowledge and my actions!

By this marvelous act He removed my difficulties, and put me into a state of innocence which resembled the innocence I remember to have had up to the age of four or five years. But I find this new innocence far more wonderful than that of childhood, which is but the innocence of ignorance. But this new innocence—which is a gift of God—is innocence with knowledge. I am not able to express the gratitude and amazement and wonder that have never ceased to fill me about this. Such things can only be spoken of by the soul to her lover, and then not in words but in a silence of tears.

What did I ever do that He should show me such kindness? I did nothing except this: I desired with all the force of my heart and soul and mind and body to love Him. I said, "Oh, if I could be the warmest, tenderest lover that ever Thou didst have! Teach me to be Thy burning lover." This was my perpetual prayer. And my idea of Heaven was and is this, that without so much as knowing, or being known or perceived by *any save Himself*, without even a name, yet retaining my full consciousness of individuality, I should be with Him for always.

Unabated Love

What is this love for God, and how define it? For myself, I never knew it until I was filled with it upon the hill. Many judge it to be a *following* of Christ and His wishes, but this is only a part of it and the way we begin it, and often we begin from duty, fear of future punishment, desire for salvation or spiritual preeminence, and obedience; and in none of these is there the joy of love.

Love is a fire, for we feel the great heat of it. Love is a light, for we perceive the white glare of it. Of things known, to what can we compare it? Most perhaps to electricity, for here we have both light and heat, and the lightning flash strikes that which already contains the most of itself (or electricity). And the lightning of God's love strikes him whose heart contains the most love for Himself. And He strikes when He will and afterwards visits when He will; and I do not count myself (for all my earthly loves) to have so much as known the outer edge of the meaning of the word love, till He struck me with His own upon that hill.

We do not love God because we do not yet know Him. And we do not know Him because we seek only to know and have our own desires: and having learnt to know these, we would have our unknown God accommodate Himself to us and them. But let us first seek to know God's desires by heart, and then accommodate our own to His: so shall we learn to be pleasing to Christ, that He may lead us, whilst here, into His Garden. For to the creature that ardently pursues God there comes at last a time when He reveals Himself to the searching soul, saying: "I Am Here. Come!" Then in secrecy we arise—and go to Him out of the House of Vanity into the music of the great Beyond.

There is small credit or virtue to the soul when, in a state of high grace or nearness, she burns with love for her God: for she is under the spell of the enticement of His Presence—how can she help but burn! It is as though two earthly lovers, in full sight and nearness, are filled each for each with great love, and are content. But this is a credit to the soul and the creature (as to the earthly lovers), that in separation and farness they should seek no other, but continue to dwell with great intentness upon the absent love. This is fidelity.

At times it is as if her Lord said to the soul: "I have other to do than to stay by thee; and also thou hast had more than enough to thy share of My honey"; and, so saying, He departs. And this is fidelity of the soul and the creature, and a great virtue, that, without change of face, without complaint or petitioning, they should with all sweetness continue to pour up to Him their unabated love. If any can do this, he is a perfect lover and has no more to learn.

Man's Impudence

Many of us are, perhaps unwittingly, impudent to God. In this way we are impudent: We question (even though it be in secret, hidden in the heart and not spoken) the justice of God, the ways of God, the plans of God, the love of God: by which means we argue with God and judge Him. And another manner of impudence we have is this, that we dare to attribute or to blame Him for the results of man's own filth, saying: "This and this is the will of God, for we see that it exists, and His will is omnipotent." Oh, beware of this impudence, drop it out of the heart and mind, and flee from it as from the plague! "How then can these things be, if He is omnipotent?" we say. Because of this, that in the trust of His great love He gave us the royal and Godly gift of freewill, and our souls have proved themselves unworthy to have it; and now the creature is brought before the Beautiful, and the Holy, and the Pure, but turning away, like the sow, prefers the mire and the festering sores proceeding from such wallowings. If there were no choice, there were no virtue, and no progress home. But let no man venture in his heart to attribute to that Holy and Marvelous Being whom we speak of as God, not knowing as yet His Name, any will towards festers and corruptions, for what does He say Himself? "Their sins rise up before Me and stink in My nostrils!"

We surely forget that this world is not yet God's Kingdom, and that His will is not done here, and will not be until the Judgment Day. This world is but a tiny testing-chamber in His mighty workshop; and great and wonderful is the care He has for the workers in it.

"Why am I here?" we cry, "to suffer all these pains, and my consent not asked? A poor, sad puppet dancing to a tune I know not the rhythm of. Where is my recompense? And where my wages? I will take all I can of what is offered here, and give no thanks! It is but my scant due for all my wretchednesses!"

O foolish man! so timid of all future possibilities of bliss that he must grasp and burn himself with such delights as he finds here! And equally mistaken and small-minded man who thinks that all our Mighty God will have to offer us hereafter are crowns, damp clouds and mists, and endless hymns! Such little hearts are far away indeed from knowing the *magnitudes of Life.*

O wretched man! why this distrust? Hast thou created even thine own palate and digestion? Hast thou invented any of those fond delights that so enslave thee now? Hast thou thyself devised the means wherewith to satisfy the longing of thy *creature* for the sweets of life? They were provided thee; all that thou hast created is misuse! Thou art but a perverted thing!—a crooked tool of self, a fly drowning in the honey that it sought too greedily to own!

O wretched, wretched man! so cloyed with sweets of earth thou canst not raise thy head to see the sunrise out beyond the world, and know true sweets! How many are the tears wept over thee by the great heart of God!

The Mystery of Music

Since coming into this new way of living, the more I come into contact with music the more I sense a mysterious connection between melody—the soul—and her *origin.* Alone out of all the sciences and arts, music has no foundation upon anything on earth. There is no music in nature until the soul, come to a perfect harmony within herself, brings out the hidden harmony in all creation, and, turning it to melody within herself, returns it to her Lord in song, whether by outward instrument or inward love. The soul, indeed, would seem to have come out of a life of infinite melody and to have dropped into an existence of mere contrary and vexing time-beat.

Who can by any means account for the variety of passions excited within him by the mere difference of the spacing, time, or rhythm of music? In my new condition of living I notice that the soul throws out with most disdainful impatience music that was formerly beautiful to my mind and heart (or my creature); and certain types of flowing cadences (very rarely to be found) sustained in high, flowing, delicate, and soaring continuity will produce in her conditions akin to a madness of joy. For one brief instant *she remembers! but cannot utter what!*

All Is One and One Is All

Of visions I know nothing, but received all my experiences into my soul as amazingly real inward perceptions. That these perceptions are of unprecedented intensity, and more realistic than those which are merely visual, can be understood by bodily comparisons; for to *feel* or to be one with fire is more than to *see* it.

To try to compare spiritual life with physical experiences would seem to be useless; for, to my feeling, while we live in the spirit we live at a great speed—indeed, an incalculably great speed—and as a whole and not in parts. For with physical living we live at one moment by the eyes, at another with the mind, at another through the heart, at another with the body. But the spirit feels to have no parts, for all parts are of so perfect a concordance that in this marvelous harmony all is one and one is all. And this with *incredible intensity*, so that we live not as now—dully—but at white heat of sensibility.

The Golden Wedding-Ring of Prayer

Prayer is the golden wedding-ring between ourselves and God. For myself, I divide it into two halves—the one petitioning, the other offering. Of petitioning I would say that this is the *work* of the soul; and of offering, that it is the pleasure of the soul; of petitioning, that I come to it under His command; and of offering, that I come to it of my own high, passionate desire. I make upon my knees, three times a day, three short and formal prayers of humble worship as befits the creature worshipping its Ineffable and Mighty God: and for the rest of my time I sing to Him from my heart and soul, as befits the joyful lover, adoring and conversing with the Ineffable and Exquisite Beloved.

We know very well that no man will find God either enclosed, held fast, or demonstrated within a circle of dogmatic words; but every man can find, in his own soul, an exquisite and incomparable instrument of communication with God. To establish the working of this communication is the whole object and meaning of life in this world—this world of material, finite, and physical things, in which the human body is at once a means and a debt.

The key to progress is a continual dressing of the will and mind and heart towards God, best brought about by continually filling the heart and mind with beautiful, grateful, and loving thoughts of Him. At all stages of progress the thoughts persistently fly away to other things in the near and visible world, and we have need quietly and perpetually to pick them up and re-center them on Him.

INDEX

For a glossary of all key foreign words used in books published by World Wisdom, including metaphysical terms in English, consult:
www.DictionaryofSpiritualTerms.org.
This on-line Dictionary of Spiritual Terms provides extensive definitions, examples, and related terms in other languages.

BIOGRAPHICAL NOTES

LILIAN STAVELEY was unknown to the public when, at the end of the First World War, she brought to John M. Watkins of London a manuscript to offer for publication. For the sake of her own privacy, she insisted upon remaining anonymous, since her beloved but non-mystical husband—Brigadier General William Cathcart Staveley of the British army—was still living, and she was surrounded by the social world she later described in her autobiography, *The Prodigal Returns*. It was only after her death that General Staveley learned that his fond wife and companion of nearly thirty years had for long led a hidden spiritual life which out of charity she had opened to the reading public in three works constituting a deeply original and grace-filled personal record of a soul's journey to God. In *The Golden Fountain* the author shares with us many secrets of a life of integral devotion, providing a marvelous example of how true mysticism leaves nothing outside the pale, but in an eminently practical manner knits up all the elements of our everyday existence into the seamless robe of contemplation.

Little is known of the author's historical person beyond the few facts she herself has told us in *The Prodigal Returns*. Born around 1878 into a distinguished and intellectual English family named Bowdoin, descended on both sides from Huguenots of the old French nobility, she was reared in an international setting, during an era when modern science seemed to promise an answer to every problem of the universe. Her discovery of a direct and living relationship with God has been chronicled in her autobiography mentioned above. It is characteristic of her spiritual way, however, that she continued to attend Anglican church services, husk though the outward form may have become for her in the light of her inward experience. She died in 1928 and her body lies buried in a Dorsetshire village.

JOSEPH A. FITZGERALD studied Comparative Religion at Indiana University, where he also earned a Doctor of Jurisprudence degree. He is a professional editor whose previous publications include *Of the Land and the Spirit: The Essential Lord Northbourne on Ecology and Religion* (with Christopher James), *Honen the Buddhist Saint: Essential Writings and Official Biography*, *The Essential Sri Anandamayi Ma: Life and Teachings of a 20th Century Saint from India*, and *The*

Cheyenne Indians: Their History and Lifeways. He lives with his wife and daughter in Bloomington, Indiana.

PHILIP ZALESKI is the author of several books, including *Prayer: A History* and *The Book of Heaven* (both with Carol Zaleski), *The Recollected Heart, Gifts of the Spirit,* and *The Best American Spiritual Writing* series. He is a research associate in Religion at Smith College.

Titles on Christianity by
World Wisdom

Chartres and the Birth of the Cathedral: Revised,
by Titus Burckhardt, 2009

Christian Spirit, edited by Judith Fitzgerald and
Michael Oren Fitzgerald, 2004

A Christian Woman's Secret: A Modern-Day Journey to God,
by Lilian Staveley, 2009

Christianity/Islam: Perspectives on Esoteric Ecumenism
A New Translation with Selected Letters,
by Frithjof Schuon, 2008

The Destruction of the Christian Tradition: Updated and Revised,
by Rama P. Coomaraswamy, 2006

For God's Greater Glory: Gems of Jesuit Spirituality,
edited by Jean-Pierre Lafouge, 2006

The Foundations of Christian Art: Illustrated,
by Titus Burckhardt, 2006

The Fullness of God: Frithjof Schuon on Christianity,
selected and edited by James S. Cutsinger, 2004

*In the Heart of the Desert, Revised: The Spirituality of the Desert Fathers and
Mothers,* by John Chryssavgis, 2008

Messenger of the Heart: The Book of Angelus Silesius,
by Angelus Silesius, 2005

Not of This World: A Treasury of Christian Mysticism,
compiled and edited by James S. Cutsinger, 2003

Paths to the Heart: Sufism and the Christian East,
edited by James S. Cutsinger, 2002

Paths to Transcendence: According to Shankara, Ibn Arabi & Meister Eckhart,
by Reza Shah-Kazemi, 2006

The Quiet Way: A Christian Path to Inner Peace,
by Gerhard Tersteegen, 2008

The Sermon of All Creation: Christians on Nature,
edited by Judith Fitzgerald and Michael Oren Fitzgerald, 2005

Siena, City of the Virgin: Illustrated,
by Titus Burckhardt, 2008

*Ye Shall Know the Truth: Christianity and
the Perennial Philosophy,*
edited by Mateus Soares de Azevedo, 2005

Titles in the Spiritual Classics Series by World Wisdom

The Buddha Eye: An Anthology of the Kyoto School and Its Contemporaries, edited by Frederick Franck, 2004

A Christian Woman's Secret: A Modern-Day Journey to God, by Lilian Staveley, 2009

Gospel of the Redman, compiled by Ernest Thompson Seton and Julia M. Seton, 2005

Introduction to Sufi Doctrine, by Titus Burckhardt, 2008

Lamp of Non-Dual Knowledge & Cream of Liberation: Two Jewels of Indian Wisdom, by Sri Swami Karapatra and Swami Tandavaraya, translated by Swami Sri Ramanananda Saraswathi, 2003

Light on the Indian World: The Essential Writings of Charles Eastman (Ohiyesa), edited by Michael Oren Fitzgerald, 2002

Music of the Sky: An Anthology of Spiritual Poetry, edited by Patrick Laude and Barry McDonald, 2004

The Mystics of Islam, by Reynold A. Nicholson, 2002

Naturalness: A Classic of Shin Buddhism, by Kenryo Kanamatsu, 2002

The Path of Muhammad: A Book on Islamic Morals and Ethics by Imam Birgivi, interpreted by Shaykh Tosun Bayrak, 2005

Pray Without Ceasing: The Way of the Invocation in World Religions, edited by Patrick Laude, 2006

The Quiet Way: A Christian Path to Inner Peace, by Gerhard Tersteegen, translated by Emily Chisholm, 2008

Tripura Rahasya: The Secret of the Supreme Goddess, translated by Swami Sri Ramanananda Saraswathi, 2002

The Way and the Mountain: Tibet, Buddhism, and Tradition, by Marco Pallis, 2008